EXPERIENCING CHOPIN

The Listener's Companion
Gregg Akkerman, Series Editor

Titles in **The Listener's Companion** provide readers with a deeper understanding of key musical genres and the work of major artists and composers. Aimed at nonspecialists, each volume explains in clear and accessible language how to *listen* to works from particular artists, composers, and genres. Looking at both the context in which the music first appeared and has since been heard, authors explore with readers the environments in which key musical works were written and performed.

EXPERIENCING CHOPIN

A Listener's Companion

Christine Lee Gengaro

ROWMAN & LITTLEFIELD
Lanham • Boulder • New York • London

Published by Rowman & Littlefield
A wholly owned subsidiary of The Rowman & Littlefield Publishing Group,
Inc.
4501 Forbes Boulevard, Suite 200, Lanham, Maryland 20706
www.rowman.com

Unit A, Whitacre Mews, 26-34 Stannary Street, London SE11 4AB

British Library Cataloguing in Publication Information Available

Library of Congress Cataloging-in-Publication Data

Names: Gengaro, Christine Lee.
Title: Experiencing Chopin : a listener's companion / Christine Lee Gengaro.
Description: Lanham : Rowman & Littlefield, [2018] | Series: Listener's companion | Includes
    bibliographical references and index.
Identifiers: LCCN 2017006652 (print) | LCCN 2017009151 (ebook) | ISBN 9781442260863
    (cloth : alk. paper) | ISBN 9781442260870 (electronic)
Subjects: LCSH: Chopin, Frédéric, 1810-1849—Criticism and interpretation. | Piano music—19th
    century—History and criticism.
Classification: LCC ML410.C54 G4 2018 (print) | LCC ML410.C54 (ebook) | DDC 786.2092—
    dc23 LC record available at https://lccn.loc.gov/2017006652

Printed in the United States of America

To my loving sister Michelle
and
To Adrian, for playing me the waltzes

CONTENTS

SERIES EDITOR'S FOREWORD

The goal of the Listener's Companion series is to give readers a deeper understanding of pivotal musical genres and the creative work of its iconic composers and performers. This is accomplished in an inclusive manner that does not necessitate extensive music training or elitist shoulder rubbing. Authors of the series place the reader in specific listening experiences in which the music is examined in its historical context with regard to both compositional and societal parameters. By positioning the reader in the real or supposed environment of the music's creation, the author provides for a deeper enjoyment and appreciation of the art form. Series authors, often drawing on their own expertise as both performers and scholars, deliver to readers a broad understanding of major musical genres and the achievements of artists within those genres as lived listening experiences.

Recent research has uncovered what is only the second known photograph of Fryderyk Chopin. In the image, his refined stature and fine clothing are quite apparent, but it is his ashen and sagging eyes that call out for attention. Are they sullen from years of illness? Buffeted by the demise of his relationship with George Sand? Defeated by the rigors of being a self-employed musician in Paris? Or is he simply tired and captured in a moment of poor lighting? The original "daguerreotype" image is suspected to have been taken in 1847, two years before Chopin's death at the age of only thirty-nine. But within that brief lifetime Chopin graced the world with a golden trove of works for the piano. Chopin, equally skilled as a composer and pianist, believed (as author Christine Gengaro will remind us in her introduction) that the "fingers should sing" as the music is being performed. And in the twenty-first century, his music still sings prominently in recital halls, salons, and theaters the world over. Be it in movies, television, academic settings, or at the community concert hall, you can expect to be regularly reminded of the dashing beauty and impassioned approach Chopin communicates through the piano.

To escort you through Chopin's robust catalog is Dr. Christine Gengaro, a historical musicologist from southern California who from her opening words will pull you in to the colorful life of the composer and his music. If you are a pianist, you will likely enjoy keeping your scores nearby, but non-performers will be likewise served by Gengaro's studied ability to reveal the essence of Chopin's music without a need for heady analytical jargon while never disrespecting the intelligence of the material at hand. After reading this much-needed entry to the Listener's Companion series and revisiting Chopin recordings, you may find someday yourself staring into the eyes of the aforementioned image, and realize that you are subtly nodding with understanding, assisted by the deft hand of Dr. Gengaro.

Gregg Akkerman

ACKNOWLEDGMENTS

Many thanks to the University of Southern California, especially the staff at the Music Library. Thanks also to the Hunter College Library (CUNY) and the Benjamin Cardozo Library (Yeshiva University). The author would like to give special recognition to David Arbury and Jessie Rothwell for their assistance. For their various contributions, the author would also like to thank Gregg Akkerman, Natalie Mandziuk, and Katie O'Brien of Rowman & Littlefield, and Diana Diskin, Cael Marcus Edwards, Michele Filorimo, Frank and Geri Gengaro, Michelle Gengaro-Kokmen, Bennett Graff, Andrea Moore, Christine Park, April Pavlik, Ryan Thompson, Jen Vaughn, and Thomas Witwer.

INTRODUCTION

Like most children born in the United States in the latter half of the twentieth century, it is likely that my first experience with Chopin occurred while I was watching a Bugs Bunny cartoon. It wasn't until years later, in college, that I started to hear the works of Chopin played for their own sake by my peers. I was immediately smitten with the waltzes, and the nocturnes and ballades cast their own spells soon after. If I'd had access to the Internet as it exists now, I likely would have spent hours on video streaming services watching the greats play my favorites. Instead, my friends and I had a decidedly low-tech way to appreciate Chopin; we held our own Romantically inspired soirées. We fancied ourselves new Bohemians, most of us music students and lovers of poetry and art. We'd dress up for potluck dinner parties (think ramen noodles and mac and cheese from the box), play Chopin, sing Schubert Lieder, and then go home to our dorm rooms and studio apartments in the New York City of the early 1990s.

To add to our fascination with Chopin and Romanticism in general, our "Bohemian" years coincided with the release of films like *Impromptu* and *Immortal Beloved*. We could also rent videotapes of older movies like *Song of Love* (about Robert Schumann), *Song Without End* (Liszt), and *A Song to Remember* (Chopin). These portrayals no doubt influenced our mental images of these composers, who in our mind's eye, began to resemble the actors who played them. Luckily, we had excellent music history professors, who were quick to remind us to take *Amadeus* and company with a grain of salt. When I ultimately went on to study musicology (after studying classical voice), it was clear that what truly fascinated me was classical music in popular culture. How do we inherit this music, and in what form does it come to us? Do we laugh at Bugs Bunny playing "Choppin's" "My-noot Waltz?" Or sing "Kill da wabbit!" along with Wagner/Elmer Fudd? Do we see Amadeus as actor Tom Hulce in perpetuity, or do we imagine the composer to look like Johann Nepomuk della Croce's famous portrait? When we hear classical music outside of the concert hall, what does it mean to us? If Chopin's music appears in a film, does it appear as part of the narrative or played in a scene, or does its presence on the soundtrack conjure images of Romantic salons, fancy soirées, or educated refinement? For our purposes here: what do Chopin and his music represent in the twenty-first century?

To my surprise and delight, I found that Chopin's music is alive and well in the ways I would have expected: it is programmed on concerts and taught in music classes and private lessons. Mastery of his piano music still implies excellence; modern pianists who can play Chopin's Études (opp. 10 and 25) are likely to have nearly all of the standard repertoire in their grasp. I was also thrilled to see that Chopin's legacy was alive in ways I hadn't expected. In chapter 10, I discuss not one, but two video games that feature Chopin as a protagonist. In both cases, Chopin's music is part of the experience. Furthermore, in the more recent game, one must play simplified versions of Chopin's pieces to battle other musicians. Schumann doesn't get to be a character in an RPG, so why does the honor go to Chopin?

Thinking back to my first (non–pop culture) forays into Chopin's work, part of the appeal for me was the sense that the music represented pure emotional expression. There was no feeling of manipulation or of Chopin imposing his own will as to how one of his pieces should make you feel. One of the things that was so prescient of Chopin was his reluctance to give his pieces catchy titles. Most of the nicknames that have traveled down to us—the "Revolutionary" Étude, the "Raindrop" Prelude—were given by other people, often publishers. The more generic titles allow us to draw out our own meanings for these works, and read our own stories into the emotional and stirring music. And, personally, to hear this music as a sensitive teenager—in a group of other sensitive teenagers—we came to feel that Chopin's music somehow understood us, in our fragile, impassioned late adolescence.

As one of the architects of the school of Romantic piano music, Chopin is the perfect remedy for the sensitive listener, who doesn't want to zone out to thoughtless music, but who wants to be emotionally engaged while actively listening.

As an educator at the college level, I teach a Chopin nocturne as part of my Music Appreciation class and several of Chopin's piano miniatures in the Music History survey curriculum. In my theory classes, I use Chopin's piano method to acquaint my students with the keyboard, especially if it's the first time they're playing. Chopin is relevant from an educational standpoint, but he's also relevant as a real human being. He suffered with physical ailments and professional and personal disappointments, and still somehow managed to create timeless works of art before his death—far too early—five months shy of his fortieth birthday. Writing this book has been an effort to speak about Chopin the human being as well as Chopin the artist. To this end, there are anecdotes and stories, information about Chopin's friends and lovers, and snapshots of his life. I haven't organized this information in a chronological way, but rather by concept. In chapter 3, for example, we explore Chopin's friendships and collaborations, in chapter 6 his love relationships, in chapter 9 his physical and mental health, and we do all of this while keeping at least one ear attuned to the music he created in these contexts. Each chapter features a discussion of a piece or set of pieces that connects back to the original concept and (hopefully) inspires you to sit back and really listen.

It has been a pleasure to immerse myself in the music of Chopin in the writing of this book, and it has been endlessly entertaining to investigate some of the stranger footnotes in Chopin's history—the fate of his heart, for example, or the spurious love letters to Delfina Potocka. It's also been quite amusing to imagine certain circumstances like a typical Chopin piano lesson or a summer day in Nohant with George Sand. In these instances, I drew upon facts of time and place, but also indulged in some invention and speculation. The overarching purpose of these sections is to shine a light on the subject as a real person and also to give the reader a reasonable picture of day-to-day life or some special event. Where possible, I used Chopin's own words from his letters, or quoted from the primary source material of his contemporaries. What emerges, I hope, is a true portrait of an actual man, touched by genius, sometimes charming, sometimes catty, incredibly unique and creative. Most of all, though, I hope this creates a greater appreciation of Chopin's music, which never fails to amaze me. The painter Eugène Delacroix once said to Chopin, "I consider you to be one of those who bring glory to our wretched species," and indeed, if Chopin can exist, perhaps there is hope for humanity after all.

TIMELINE

1810   Chopin is born on March 1 (or February 22, based on the baptismal record) in Żelazowa Wola, Poland to Mikołaj (Nicholas) and Justyna Chopin. His older sister Ludwika was born in 1807; in October, the family moves to Warsaw so Mikołaj can work at the Warsaw Lyceum

1811   Chopin's younger sister Izabela is born

1812   Chopin's father begins teaching French language and literature at the School of Artillery and Engineering; Chopin's youngest sister, Emilia, is born

1814   Chopin's father receives an appointment to teach French literature at the Lyceum

1816   Chopin begins formal lessons with Wojciech Żywny

1817   The Chopin family moves to apartments at the Kazimierz Palace; Chopin composes his first works including a Polonaise in B-flat major (written in his father's hand), a march, and variations (now lost); another piece, the Polonaise in G minor, is published, dedicated to Viktoria Skarbek

1818   Chopin receives his first review in the press; in February, he plays a benefit concert where he performs a concerto by Vojtech Jírovec; Chopin plays two of his compositions for the mother of the tsar

1819   The young composer is very much in demand by the
             aristocracy, including Grand Duke Constantine, who enjoys
             his playing

1822   Chopin ends his study with Żywny and begins to take
             composition lessons with Józef Elsner and organ lessons with
             Wilhelm Václav Würfel

1823   Plays at a few soirées and at one, performs a concerto by
             Ferdinand Ries; at another, the Fifth Concerto of John Field

1824   Spends the summer holidays in Szafarnia with a friend,
             Dominik "Domus" Dziewanowski; he hears folk music in the
             countryside; his first letters to his parents date from this time,
             showing him to be clever, self-possessed, and charming; he
             may have sung in the Christmas choir at the Augsburg
             Evangelical Church

1825   The *Kurier Warszawski* reports that Chopin was given a
             diamond ring from Tsar Alexander I after a performance; the
             Rondo in C minor becomes Chopin's first published work
             with an opus number; summer holidays in Szafarnia; enjoys a
             performance of Rossini's *Barber of Seville* and composes a
             work, now lost, on a theme from the opera; plays organ for
             the school

1826   Suffers from swollen glands and other symptoms; the doctor
             pronounces a catarrhal affliction, and Chopin is bled with
             leeches; Fryderyk and younger sister Emilia are taken to a
             spa for their health; finishes his study at the Lyceum;
             performs at some charitable events; continues studies with
             Elsner under the auspices of the Szkoła Głowna Muzyki
             (where Elsner is a faculty member); composes the Rondo à la
             Mazur in F major, op. 5

1827   Attends a performance by the pianist Maria Szymanowska at
             the National Theater; in February, Emilia dies of
             consumption; the family moves to a different home; Chopin
             composes the Variations on a Theme from Mozart's "La ci
             darem la mano" and dedicates it to friend Tytus
             Wojciechowski; a couple of his works are sent to Leipzig for
             publication

1828   The death of childhood friend Jan Białobłocki from tuberculosis; Chopin attends a performance by Johann Nepomuk Hummel and sees Rossini's *Otello*; summer holidays at Sanniki nad Wisła with friend Konstanty Pruszak; in September he takes his first trip abroad to Berlin; experiences the musical culture of the city including several operas; returns home with a stop in Poznań; plays numerous salons and private performances

1829   Meets Konstancja Gładowska at a concert; sees Paganini in concert; finishes formal study at the Szkoła Główna Muzyki; in July he makes his first trip to Vienna where he attends many concerts and operas; performs two concerts at the Kärntnerthortheater at the behest of organ teacher Würfel; makes the acquaintance of many important musical figures in the city; both concerts are very well received; passes through Prague and Teplice, where he plays at a musical soirée; visits Dresden for a week before returning to Warsaw; attends the informal Friday concerts at the home of Józef Kessler; begins writing études

1830   Presents the F minor Concerto at his first public concert in Warsaw, at the National Theater; reviews are positive, although there is talk that Chopin's playing is too quiet for large spaces; a second concert follows five days later; Chopin works on the E minor Concerto; watches Gładowska's stage debut in July; begins dabbling in song writing; in October, Chopin plays his farewell concert at the National Theater; he plays the E minor Concerto and the *Fantasy on Polish Airs*; in November he leaves Warsaw; he travels with Tytus Wojciechowski through Dresden and Prague to Vienna; after the November Uprising, Tytus returns to Poland, but Chopin stays in Vienna; renews old friendships and makes new acquaintances including Anton Diabelli and theorist Maximilian Stadler; his first Christmas away from family is somewhat melancholy

1831   Plays at a musical matinee benefit concert in April; in May, spends time at the residence of physician and music lover Johann Malfatti; performs at the Kärntnerthortheater in

June, presenting the Concerto in E minor; writes songs for voice and piano during the summer; leaves Vienna after eight months; arrives in Paris in September; meets members of the Paris music scene including Kalkbrenner and Rossini; meets lifelong friend Delfina Potocka; meets and later collaborates with Auguste Franchomme on the Variations on a Theme from *Robert le diable*; Robert Schumann's favorable review of Variations on "La ci darem la mano" appears in December

1832   Unfavorable review of "La ci darem la mano" published by Ludwig Rellstab; in February, Chopin makes his Parisian debut at the Salle Pleyel; summer in Tours with Franchomme; in the winter, hears performances by John Field

1833   Kalkbrenner composes a set of Variations on a Theme from Chopin's Mazurka in B-flat major (op. 7, no. 1); he plays solo works and pieces with Liszt and Hiller in numerous salons; deepening friendship with Liszt; Chopin's works begin to be published in England; Rellstab prints a scathing review of the mazurkas

1834   Chopin participates in musical salons and soirées with Hiller, Vincenzo Bellini, and Liszt; Rellstab negatively reviews the op. 10 Études; Chopin's father worries about his son overburdening himself; short visit to the country with Berlioz, Liszt, Hiller, and Alfred de Vigny; meets Felix Mendelssohn; becomes roommates with Jan Matuszyński; participates in a benefit concert for Harriet Smithson (wife of Berlioz); plays a concert on Christmas with Liszt in the showroom of Stoepel

1835   Chopin helps to organize a benefit concert for Polish orphans; Chopin plays the Concerto in E minor, and many other musicians participate, including Liszt; in April, Chopin performs in his last public concert for many years; Chopin in talks with Breitkopf & Härtel for the publication of works including the op. 27 Nocturnes, the op. 25 Études, and the op. 26 Polonaises; sees his parents at Karlsbad for what will be the last time in August; relationship with Maria Wodzińska; sees Robert Schumann, Felix Mendelssohn, and

Clara Wieck in Leipzig; experiences a health crisis at the end of the year leading to a rumor of his death

1836   Chopin falls ill again in the spring; Schumann reviews Chopin's Concertos; numerous works published in Leipzig; spends a month in Marienbad with the Wodziński family; tentative engagement between Chopin and Maria Wodzińska, contingent upon Chopin's improved health; meets Schumann in Leipzig; in October, meets George Sand for the first time; his first impression is unfavorable; Sand, Liszt, and Countess Marie d'Agoult (romantic partner of Liszt) participate in a musical soirée at Chopin's home; Chopin acts as a witness at Jan Matuszyński's wedding; childhood friend Julian Fontana and student Adolf Gutmann become copyists for Chopin's work

1837   Contact with the Wodziński family tapers off; Sand repeatedly invites Chopin to her home in Nohant, but he does not accept; Chopin does not perform with Liszt at the Salle Erard because of illness; in July, travels to London for two weeks; dedicates the op. 25 Études to Marie d'Agoult

1838   Performs at a few small salons of friends; in May or June Sand and Chopin begin their intimate relationship; in October, the two travel (separately) to spend the winter in Mallorca together; in November, Chopin becomes very sick; they take residence at a Carthusian monastery in Valldemosa after fears of Chopin's illness force them to leave the inn at Palma; bad weather and difficult conditions provide challenges, but Chopin continues to compose the Preludes and other works

1839   Chopin's Pleyel piano finally arrives from Paris; Chopin asks Fontana to conduct business matters for him; in Barcelona, Chopin has another health crisis during which he coughs up blood; he recovers over three months in Marseilles; Chopin dedicates the op. 40 Polonaises to Fontana for all of his help; vacation with Sand to Genoa; productive summer spent in Nohant with Sand: Chopin composes a scherzo, a nocturne, and a sonata; the Preludes op. 28 are dedicated to Pleyel; the Ballade in F major is dedicated to Schumann; in October,

Chopin returns to Paris and to teaching; plays a private concert with Ignaz Moscheles; negotiates with Breitkopf & Härtel for an increased rate of pay for a dozen new works

1840   Enjoys socializing with Sand and his Parisian friends; falls ill in April; works from the summer in Nohant begin to be published; plays at the home of Marquis de Custine; becomes friends with Pauline Viardot and her husband Louis; Chopin contributes three études to Moscheles and Fetís's *Piano Method*; attends poet Adam Mickiewicz's lectures at the College de France

1841   Sand publishes her book about the winter in Mallorca; attends a concert by Viardot with Sand and painter Eugène Delacroix; in February he suffers with health issues and coughs up blood; Chopin gives a recital at the Salle Pleyel for considerable financial gain; Liszt publishes a thoughtful review of Chopin's work; Sand and Chopin stay in Nohant from June to November; the Viardots visit Nohant in August; Chopin spends another productive few months writing music in Nohant; makes many demands on Fontana including a new place to live for himself, Sand, and her children; returns to Paris in November

1842   The first part of Sand's novel *Consuelo* (reportedly inspired by Pauline Viardot) is published; performs with Viardot at a concert at the Conservatoire; performs at the Salle Pleyel in February; suffers from rheumatism in March; witnesses the death of Jan Matuszyński; Chopin and Sand spend May through September at Nohant; in July, Chopin takes a short trip to Paris with Sand to choose a new place to live; continues teaching and acquiring new students; one student, Carl Filtsch, shows great promise at the age of twelve

1843   Health crisis in February; probably participates in a benefit concert for Fontana; Carl Filtsch plays Chopin's F minor Concerto at the Salle Erard; Sand and Chopin spend May through October in Nohant; visit to Paris in August to deal with publisher Schlésinger; sends manuscripts bound for London to banker Auguste Léo; returns to Paris to teach, among others, Jane Stirling and Camille O'Meara; Chopin falls ill in November; Sand turns forty; signs contract with Breitkopf & Härtel for rights to the publication of 33 opus numbers

1844   Health problems in January; plays short recital for Bohdan Zaleski; concert by Gutmann; death of Chopin's father; sister Ludwika visits Paris; summer in Nohant; corresponds with Franchomme about business matters; Ludwika's departure is treated with a soirée with performances by Chopin and Franchomme; returns to Paris for lessons, while Sand stays in Nohant

1845   Suffers from "asthma" in March; Carl Filtsch dies in May at fourteen; plays a soirée at the Paris residence of Duke and Duchess Czartoryski; summer in Nohant with Pauline Viardot and others; tensions rise between Chopin and Sand's son Maurice; in September, visit to Paris to talk to his own publishers and Sand's as well; in December, Liszt gives concerts in Paris and visits with Chopin

1846   Spends a week in Tours recovering from an illness; Sand and Chopin spend the summer in Nohant; Sand's novel *Lucrezia Floriani* is published; Chopin's productivity slows; Grzymała visits Nohant; other visitors to Nohant include Pauline Viardot and Delacroix; returns to Paris in November

1847   Performs at a soirée at Delfina Potocka's; completes the Cello Sonata, op. 65; Sand returns to Nohant in April; Solange Sand becomes engaged to sculptor Clésinger; George Sand begins writing her memoir; health crisis in May; well enough to attend the wedding at Nohant; Chopin holds a soirée at his home including Grzymała and Franchomme; Chopin helps Solange Sand, estranging himself from George; the Sand/Chopin relationship ends in late July

1848   Suffers with the flu while preparing a concert; February, Chopin's final concert in Paris in the Salle Pleyel; February Revolution breaks out; Chopin's students dwindle; Solange gives birth to a daughter, who dies in a week; final chance encounter with Sand; spends seven months in England and Scotland, arranged by Jane Stirling; plays many concerts,

some public, some in private residences; health problems in
October; last public concert; return to Paris in November

1849   Takes on no new students; sees Delacroix and Potocka
frequently; Sand asks Viardot to report on the condition of
Chopin's health; summer in Chaillot; cholera outbreak in
Paris; health crisis in June; Chopin requests Ludwika visit
him and she arrives in August; receives many visitors in
September including Franchomme, Jane Stirling, and
Duchess Czartoryska; makes final requests as to what to do
after his death; friends surround Chopin in his final hours,
among them, Gutmann and Potocka; Chopin dies on October
17; funeral services take place in the church of St. Magdalen,
and Chopin is buried at Père-Lachaise cemetery

I

THE PIANO LESSON

The experience of learning the piano, or even of trying to learn, stays with people all their lives. It affects their posture; physical coordination; relations with parents, siblings, and children; self-discipline and self-confidence; capacity to learn from others and from their own mistakes; capacity to listen, read, process, and think; and ability to speak, move, act—and play—in public.
> —"The Piano Lesson," E. Douglas Bomberger, Martha Dennis Burns, James Parakilas, Judith Tick, Marina Tsvetaeva, and Mark Tucker

It is an overcast morning in Paris in the late autumn of 1847. Renowned pianist, composer, and teacher Fryderyk Chopin wakes early in anticipation of a full day. He prepares an outfit from his always fashionable wardrobe, achieving a look that could easily be described as understated elegance. His health, never reliable even in his youth, is all right this morning. He has five students scheduled for this day, a typical workday for Chopin during this time of year. Lessons run about forty-five minutes to an hour for the average student. On Sundays—when he sees his most gifted students—a single lesson might run to three hours. But today, he has planned to see five students, and perhaps, if there is time later, he might compose for a bit or go out with friends.

For this day of work, Chopin will earn one hundred gold francs, twenty from each of his students. Many students come weekly at their appointed time, while the most ambitious (and well off) can afford to come more often. On another day, an aristocratic lady might send a coach to pick up Chopin so that he might teach her at her home. She would pay an extra ten francs for this privilege. And although the price of the opportunity to study with one of the geniuses of Romantic piano music was ostensibly fixed, and well within the budget of the elite class that mostly made up Chopin's students, there are many accounts of Chopin offering discounts or teaching extra lessons for which he did not charge. In 1847, the average worker in Paris earned just one franc a day, so a single lesson with Chopin was close to what an average worker would earn over a number of weeks.

As the rooms of Chopin's apartment warm in anticipation of his first student, he might play for a few moments on the large Pleyel piano in the center of the room. He will give this seat to the student upon her arrival, and take his place at the small upright *pianino* set up next to the Pleyel. He is always fastidiously punctual and fully dedicated to teaching. Even when his health is poor, he hardly ever cancels lessons, preferring to continue teaching even if it means lying down in the adjoining room and calling out directives to his pupils.

Chopin is much sought after as a teacher; his reputation in Paris is quite favorable. It's very difficult to make contact with him, however, since he often goes out with an entourage of sorts, who don't allow just anyone near. He teaches neither children nor beginners. There are, of course, exceptions to this rule, but they are rare. As he teaches, Chopin is taking the experiences he has and turning them into a method for piano, a side project that he writes and adds to over time, but will sadly never finish.

When his student, an aristocratic woman, arrives, she doffs her coat and sits down at the Pleyel. Chopin listens to her play. Perhaps he asks her to begin with some exercises assigned from Muzio Clementi. He listens to the sound of her fingers on the keys; he tries to hear the way she plays the notes, not just the notes themselves. He remarks that there is no substitute for the suppleness of technique. He writes in his *Projet de Méthode*, "One needs only to study a certain positioning of the hand in relation to the keys to obtain with ease the most beautiful quality of sound, to know how to play long notes and short notes, and [to attain] unlimited dexterity." Once he is satisfied with the exercises, Chopin asks her to move on to a Prelude and Fugue from J. S. Bach's *Well-Tempered Clavier*. Chopin is quite fond of the work of Bach. Bach's pieces require precision, an attention to detail that Chopin values in not only his own playing but also in that of his students. Perhaps the student stumbles on a passage. Chopin plays the same passage from his *pianino*, offering a model of how it should be done. He is, for the most part, very patient with his students. Chopin simply demonstrates and the student tries to match his extraordinary technique. There are of course some stories of Chopin losing patience, but those are few and far between. Technical matters are of great importance, but so is expression. Chopin is also quite taken with the idea of suggesting that the pianist must "sing with the fingers," a suggestion he repeated often to Émilie von Gretsch (née von Timm), who took more than thirty lessons with Chopin.

Less than an hour after its beginning, the lesson begins to wrap up. Perhaps Chopin assigns a new piece or encourages more work on something else, but he never puts undue pressure on his students to play for long periods. In fact, Chopin is adamant that a student practice no more than three hours a day. Any more might cause tension or stress, two things that ruin a student's "suppleness" in performance.

Overall, Chopin aims to explain as clearly as possible what he's looking for in the execution of a piece. When the clear demonstration is not enough, he may use imagery to inspire an emotional connection; perhaps he will even read an appropriately evocative passage from literature. Within sixty minutes, the lesson is over, Chopin receives his payment (the student leaves it discreetly on the mantelpiece so no business transactions sully the lesson), and he takes a short break, waiting for his next student to arrive.

From 1832 to 1849, this routine was repeated, almost daily, from October to May: Chopin's teaching season, if you will. The spring and summer were often spent elsewhere, outside of Paris, where he could concentrate on composition. The arrangement was not ideal, of course, as Chopin's creative instincts were pushed aside for half of the year, but lessons were his primary source of income, and it was simply a necessity that he maintain such a schedule.

Five students made up a full day, although there were times he saw more than that. In his later years—and he by no means lived to be an old man, we're talking late thirties here—he took it a little easier, but still kept up a brisk business, even with all of the health problems he experienced. Rather than being put out by his pedagogical duties, he was by all accounts a spectacular teacher, demonstrating passion and patience and a focus on success. One student, Karol Mikuli, described his teacher as experiencing "veritable joy" in the lessons, helping his students realize their potential with "a holy artistic zeal . . . and every word from his lips was stimulating and a source of enthusiasm."

The focus of this chapter is Fryderyk Chopin the teacher, but in order to explain Chopin's work as a pedagogue, we must delve into the context of musical life in the nineteenth century. Central to this discussion is the piano itself, the instrument that Chopin chose as his voice, and the instrument that had a place in most middle and upper-class homes by the early nineteenth century. Chopin's own musical education is part of this story, with his early teachers not only providing him with a strong foundation in both technique and style, but also laying the groundwork for Chopin's future as a pedagogue. In addition, we discuss one of the composers most often assigned by Chopin the teacher, the so-called Father of the Piano, Muzio Clementi. Finally, the chapter concludes with an exploration of Chopin's Études, a genre specifically designed as a pedagogical tool. In the twenty-seven études that Chopin completed in his career, the composer used his considerable talent to write pieces that were clever teaching tools that also happened to be musically brilliant and innovative. Some of the Études are quite challenging, indeed, and a thorough study of them reveals many important aspects of technique that Chopin imparted to his students. Chopin may be gone, but his Études are still teaching lessons.

CHOPIN THE TEACHER

We know Chopin the teacher through a few important sources. First and foremost is the primary source of Chopin's sketches for his *Projet de Méthode*. In this document are many ideas, including what might be viewed as a philosophical discussion of what music actually is:

- The art that manifests itself through sound is called music.
- The art of expressing one's thoughts through sounds.
- The art of handling sounds.
- Thought expressed through sounds.
- The expression of our perceptions through sounds.

- The expression of our thought through sounds.
- The manifestation of our feelings through sounds.
- The indefinite (indeterminate) language of men is sound.
- The indefinite language music.
- Word is born of sound—sound before word.
- Word[:] a certain modification of sound.

In addition to the more philosophical, Chopin also included such pedestrian things as the values of notes and rests, and an explanation of the staff as a ladder that shows the notes as steps that go up or down. Moreover, he explained that the proper position of the pianist was at the center of the keyboard, with the elbows on the same level as the white keys, and hands whose fingers point directly forward.

In addition to the *Projet de Méthode*, which was unfortunately only a few pages of sketches rather than a fully fleshed-out manual, we have recollections of many of his students in the form of letters, journals, and even books. We have some musical scores with notations made by Chopin. Finally, we have Chopin's own diaries and personal albums, and extensive correspondence both by Chopin and about him.

As Chopin taught, year after year, his reputation as both a composer and a teacher grew. His genius at the piano as a performer was also well known, although he did not often perform publicly. The only other person who approached this level of mastery in piano performance, composition, and pedagogy was Franz Liszt. Liszt was a dynamic performer and an adventurous composer (more so than Chopin), but he was not the teacher that Chopin was. Liszt, however, boasted more famous pupils. Chopin limited himself to teaching advanced students and some less experienced students who showed great potential. If a Polish student asked for lessons, he or she would likely be given priority as Chopin had a soft spot for his fellow countrymen and women. It also appears that Chopin enjoyed teaching women slightly more than he enjoyed teaching men, although he had plenty of male students. He did not work with children, but he made exceptions in exceptional cases, like eleven-year-old Carl Filtsch, fifteen-year-old Adolf Gutmann, and teen Maria von Harder.

Maria von Harder was an exceptional young pianist of Russian and German descent. She came to Paris in 1847, and was first discouraged by Chopin who told Maria's mother, Maria Alexandrowna, that he did not teach children. But she was not to be dissuaded, and Chopin met with young Maria frequently, for the whole of his teaching season. Chopin treated her as he would an adult, expecting the very best from her and not showing leniency because of her tender age. Later, Maria would recount details of these lessons to Sophie von Adelung: "Nothing escaped the sharpness of his hearing and his vision; he gave every detail the keenest attention." Even when he was too ill to stand or even sit, his senses were still finely attuned to his students. Maria von Harder remembers that he displayed an almost superhuman ability to listen: "'Fourth finger on F-sharp!', he would call out; his ear, sensitive to the slightest nuance, knew immediately, from the sound, which finger had played the note."

Chopin was rather deeply occupied with the hand and the fingers, and the best way to use them when playing. In his method, he reasons that the first scale we are all taught to play (even today)—C major—is the one least natural for the hand. Chopin instead suggested beginning with E major or B major, scales that allow the shorter fingers to sit on white keys, while the longer fingers naturally fall on the black keys. Because of the keyboard's design, this position also introduces the graceful curve of the hand encouraged by piano teachers everywhere. Furthermore, Chopin took pains to discuss the "particular charm" of each finger; the thumb being built for power, the third acting as a pivot, the fourth's literal attachment to the third by a ligament, the fifth finger as the opposite of the thumb. Only in addressing these differences and learning with them in mind can a player develop. It seems Chopin's concern was matching up, whenever possible, the design of the hand with the design of the instrument. He endeavored to make these connections in the music he wrote, and chose repertoire for his students that reflected this relationship to a certain extent.

THE PIANO IN THE NINETEENTH CENTURY

For much of the eighteenth century, the dominant keyboard was the harpsichord. It was often used as a supportive instrument within ensembles that would hold harmonies together (along with a bass instrument) while the solo instruments played more intricate lines. This combination of the harpsichord (or sometimes another instrument capable of playing multiple notes at once) and bass instrument was called the *basso continuo*. This two-instrument entity sat at the heart of most Baroque ensembles. The harpsichord was often therefore thought of as an instrument of service, rather than one of soloistic possibility, but the harpsichord occasionally emerged from its supportive role to sit in the spotlight as a soloist. Certainly the wealth of solo keyboard literature grew as the years progressed. J. S. Bach very notably gave the instrument a scintillating solo part in one of his Brandenburg Concertos, but by and large, its main duties were to round out the sound of a Baroque ensemble and fill out the harmonies over which the solo instruments played.

One thing the harpsichord lacked was the ability to change dynamics. The mechanism of the instrument is a plectrum plucking a string, and the keys that activate this mechanism are not touch sensitive. A harder tap on the keys will not result in an appreciably louder sound; the dynamic range of the plucking was minimal. The range of the harpsichord was about two octaves smaller than what we are used to on the modern piano.

Bartolomeo Cristofori is credited with the invention of the piano, which he called *gravicembalo col piano e forte*, which was later called *pianoforte*, which then became just *piano*. The name of the instrument referred to the ability to play quietly (*piano*, in Italian) and loudly (*forte*). Although the exact date is uncertain, three of Cristofori's early instruments from the 1720s survive. The pianos built in Vienna in the mid- to late-eighteenth century were constructed with wooden frames across which the strings for each pitch (two per note) were stretched. The key color was not standardized, and some pianos had black natural keys and white accidentals. The mechanism for sound production was not a plectrum, but instead a leather-covered hammer that would hit the string when a key was struck. This new instrument demonstrated dynamic and expressive possibilities that had previously been impossible.

The methods for playing piano, consequently, had to address the new dynamic possibilities, and the pedagogical exercises written for the instrument likewise had to take these things into account. While a harpsichordist might have sat a bit closer to the instrument if it had a second keyboard—called a manual—that was set higher and further back than the main manual, a pianist's body position had to respond to a longer keyboard (and its expanded range), allowing for the arms of the player to reach the extreme highs and lows of the instrument with ease. The greater physical force used when playing passages *fortissimo* would have also been a consideration. Fingering for the new instrument was also a topic for discussion. Before J. S. Bach, keyboard players used the middle three fingers primarily, but the complexity of Bach's music required facility in all of the fingers. The pre-Bach common practice included finger crossings we would consider exceedingly inconvenient, like crossing the index finger over the third finger in scales. No modern piano teacher would allow this, partially because the modern method has been in place for so long, but also, the size and weight of piano keys makes it impractical. In 1753, Bach's son, Carl Philipp Emmanuel Bach, wrote a treatise for playing keyboard instruments which sought to "develop a sound, systematic basis for fingering." This new method included the primary use of the thumb in scales and chords. Another early method book from 1797 by Johann Peter Milchmeyer, called *Die wahre Art das Pianoforte zu spielen* (*The correct method of playing the pianoforte*) has illustrations depicting the proper "rounded finger position" we still impart to our students today.

Further technological developments in the piano brought stronger frames made of cast iron, strung with high-tensile steel wires. The leather hammer coverings were replaced by coverings made of felt. The range of the instrument grew from the five octaves available to Mozart to five and a half octaves in the 1790s. By 1820, the range of the piano had grown to seven octaves. This is the piano that was available to fifty-year-old Beethoven and ten-year-old Chopin.

As the music of pianist/composers like Chopin and Franz Liszt gained popularity, virtuosity itself became the ultimate goal. The development of the Conservatory system in Europe in the nineteenth century aligned itself with the trends in piano composition, and it was the training of new virtuosos that occupied the piano programs of the Conservatories. To this end, rigorous pedagogical systems were devised, and such techniques have continued through the subsequent centuries.

Many piano students by the end of the eighteenth century were women, even if most of these women would not have been encouraged to become publicly performing virtuosos. It was an interesting paradox. Women were encouraged to learn the instrument, and for a very long time, piano lessons were all but expected for ladies of a certain class. As the nineteenth century progressed, some of these women worked very hard to achieve levels of mastery and virtuosity that they were never going to use for any professional purpose. They would simply be virtuosic players who played for the guests that came to their homes or for their family's entertainment. The Paris Conservatoire proved ahead of its time by accepting women in the early nineteenth century and allowing them to study piano, but they balked at offering them advanced theory and composition lessons. The prevailing attitude held that women were incapable of writing music, only playing it. And when it came time for competitions, the women and men were rated separately.

Some believed women were fine interpreters of music, as long as the pursuit remained a hobby. To these people, it was unseemly for a woman of marrying age to eschew traditional family life to pursue music. Most young ladies who studied piano seriously either gave up their lessons upon marriage or pregnancy, or at the very least attended fewer lessons. One need only to think of the sisters of two great musical child prodigies for examples. Maria Anna "Nannerl" Mozart, older sister of Wolfgang Amadeus Mozart, was a skilled musician from childhood. It was both she and her famous younger brother who were ferried about Europe, entertaining members of the noble class. But by the time she was seventeen, her father forbade her from continuing to play in public, as she had reached the age when young women were supposed to marry, have children, and run a home. Felix Mendelssohn, too, had a musically talented older sister, Fanny. When the two siblings attended the Sing-Akademie zu Berlin, Carl Friedrich Zelter—head of the school—praised Fanny's piano technique by saying, "she plays like a man." When she reached a marriageable age, her father told her flatly that music could only be an "ornament" and not her profession. She married and had one son, but she continued to play privately, and she also composed. A few of her works were published under Felix's name in his Opus 8 and Opus 9 collections.

Women in the nineteenth century—those of a certain leisure and elite class—were expected to play well for no other reason than it was the fashion. As Nancy Reich states in her essay "Women as Musicians," a degree from a conservatory "was a prize that could be an asset in the marriage market, [and] attested to competence." Teaching these women was a lucrative business. They were trained more or less the same as their male counterparts, and taken to the very same heights of virtuosity—to a point. Eventually, most women hit a glass ceiling beyond which they would not progress. Many were told "that they would never be ready—to play pieces of the very sort that they had been trained to play."

The majority of Chopin's students were women from this elite class. Many displayed considerable talent, but the prevailing attitudes of the day allowed their public performances only at charity events and the like. Two extraordinary students of Chopin, Friederike Streicher (née Müller) and Emilie von Gretsch (née von Timm), ceased their formal musical study when they married. Others did not become performers, but instead went on to careers in pedagogy: Vera de Rubio (née Kologrivoff) and Camille Dubois (née O'Meara) became private teachers. There were approximately ten male pupils of Chopin who went on to a career in performance. The best known of this group are Karol Mikuli and Georges Mathias. But perhaps this small number was not an accident of fate, but more in line with Chopin's own principles. As a pianist who preferred to avoid formal public performance, perhaps he consciously favored training pianists who would perform in the intimate environs of salons and private homes. One female student recalls Chopin saying, "concerts are never real music; you have to give up the idea of hearing in them the most beautiful things of art."

For families in the elite class, the piano was the center of the home. In the previous century, piano lessons were not the formal, scheduled events that they became in the Romantic period. If we go back to the example of Mozart, we see him learning his keyboard skills from his father, who was in the family business of music. If we go back even further to J. S. Bach, we see a musician taught music not just by his father, but by other relatives. This meant that lessons were likely less formal (we meet every Tuesday at 4:00), and more ongoing (let's practice a bit before dinner). If a young student was taught by someone outside of the family, it was possible that lessons were happening as often as daily. And if the lessons happened daily, there likely wasn't much practice time available. Chopin's contemporary and fellow composer, teacher, and pianist, Carl Czerny (1791–1857)—whose piano exercises are still used in schools and private lessons today—recommended that a student practice three hours a day. These hours were broken down into a half hour of exercises, an hour going over old pieces, and the remainder for learning new pieces. Exercises, in this case, meant scales and études.

Creating and selling these exercises and études became a business venture for many young performer/composers. Those who relied on teaching as a steady source of income often wrote exercises for their students anyway, so why not publish a collection to further one's own reputation? Also, these collections were building up a body of literature that addressed the piano as a solo instrument with its emerging dynamic and expressive possibilities.

FATHER OF THE PIANO

Among the repertoire assigned by Chopin to his students were études by Johann Baptist Cramer, works by Bach, sonatas by Beethoven, and nocturnes by John Field and by Chopin himself. Chopin was particularly fond of assigning exercises by the composer known as "the father of the piano." Muzio Clementi was an Italian-born composer who spent a good part of his career in England. His style as a keyboard player grew out of two main influences: the late Baroque harpsichord technique of Domenico Scarlatti and the early Classical pieces of Johann Christian Bach (one of Johann Sebastian Bach's sons). From Scarlatti he learned precision; from J. C. Bach, he learned the art of legato playing. (In legato playing, the notes feel connected, which is especially difficult on the piano, an instrument that relies on a hammer hitting a string to produce sound.) The moniker "father of the piano" refers to Clementi's sensitivity to the unique features of the piano, and indeed, his op. 2 sonatas seem to show a new direction for the instrument. Some consider these sonatas to be the beginning of a piano style that values virtuosity, a legacy that Chopin, Liszt, and Rachmaninoff would inherit.

Clementi's musical talent was apparent early; he became church organist in his hometown by the time he was thirteen. An Englishman named Peter Beckford heard Clementi play and brought him back to England, specifically an estate in Dorset, where Clementi studied the harpsichord and wrote music. Seven years later, the composer moved to London. In 1780 he set off on his first European tour, and on Christmas Eve of 1781 in Vienna, Clementi met Mozart, and the two engaged in a piano contest for the pleasure of Emperor Joseph II. They were asked to play some of their own pieces, improvise, and read pieces at sight. Emperor Joseph, ever the diplomat, declared the contest a draw. From the experience, Clementi gained a positive impression of Mozart, noting specifically the "spirit and grace" of his playing. Mozart, however, remained unimpressed with Clementi; in a letter to his father, Mozart dismissed his contemporary as "a mere mechanicus."

In the last quarter of the eighteenth century, Clementi found great success in London, playing his own works, composing, and teaching. Like Chopin after him, Clementi was a sought-after teacher, instructing many important students, among them, John Field (see chapter 4). Dubious sources had him teaching upward of sixteen hours a day. While this figure is certainly inflated, it is true that Clementi taught a great deal and charged a very high fee for his lessons.

Clementi invested some of his fortune in music publishing and in the manufacture of instruments, specifically the pianoforte. In 1801, Clementi published his method on piano playing: *Introduction to the Art of Playing on the Pianoforte*. It is from this method and from his many piano pieces that he is best known today. Clementi's *Six Progressive Sonatinas*, op. 36, are often assigned to piano students. Their popularity has persisted for the two centuries since their publication. As Clementi biographer Leon Plantinga explains: "In these bright, brief pieces the texture has been distilled until only what is essential remains; all attention is focused on the most basic issues in piano playing: clear phrasing, evenness of touch, and control of dynamics." In addition, Clementi also assembled the three-volume *Gradus ad Parnassum*, an album of a hundred works published over the years 1817, 1819, and 1826. Some of the pieces Clementi included in the collection dated back decades. Clementi included exercises—some of which clearly explained their pedagogical purpose, and preludes, fugues, and other short pieces. Plantinga noted, "A fair impression of Clementi's accomplishments as a composer can be gained from these copious volumes." Debussy immortalized Clementi in his *Children's Corner* suite from 1908, by including a movement called Dr. Gradus ad Parnassum. But far from being simply a didactic tool of emotionless exercises, Clementi infused even his most pedagogical works with a sense of artfulness.

Clementi lived from 1752 to 1832, his lifetime spanning from before Mozart's birth in 1756 to after Beethoven's death in 1827. He knew Haydn, Mozart, and Beethoven. His career covered a significant por-

tion of both the Classical and the Romantic periods and his compositions range from the simple clarity so prevalent at mid-eighteenth century to the Romantic musings of expressive piano music that Chopin
would come to dominate. We can see a kinship in their skillful use of
counterpoint and their virtuosic phrasing. It seems no great leap to
surmise that these two aspects are what Chopin found so interesting
about Clementi's work. It may have also provided Chopin with the next
logical musical step after the work of J. S. Bach, which Chopin deeply
respected.

Although today Clementi is known primarily as a composer of pedagogical piano music, he was a prolific writer of orchestral music as well.
Unfortunately, his orchestral work paled in comparison to that of his
contemporaries. Who could have hoped to have competed with the
likes of Haydn (during his London period) and Beethoven? Clementi's
symphonies would fade into obscurity, but the impact of his keyboard
method and exercises would continue to reverberate still today.

CHOPIN'S FIRST TEACHERS

All of the members of the Chopin family shared a love of music. Chopin's eldest sister, Ludwika, learned piano as a child and taught what
she knew to her younger siblings. When young Fryderyk exhausted her
knowledge, he began lessons with his mother, Justyna (née Krzyza-
nowska). By the time he had reached school age, he'd already moved
past what his mother could teach him and so required lessons from
outside of the home. As the Chopins resided in Warsaw by this time—
with Chopin's father, Mikołaj teaching literature and French at the
Warsaw Lyceum—young Chopin was introduced to sixty-year-old Wojciech Żywny. Żywny boasted that he himself had studied with a student
who had studied with J. S. Bach. This alleged direct line to Bach proved
very important to Chopin, who was introduced to the works of the High
Baroque master in his lessons. In the six years Żywny worked with
young Fryderyk, he made two contributions to Chopin's development;
the first was his emphasis on the works of Bach as a pedagogical tool,
and second was his recognition of Chopin's nascent genius that he allowed to develop without constraint. The former began Chopin's love
affair with Bach's music—specifically his counterpoint—that would al-

ways stay with the composer, while the latter preserved the unique style
of playing that would influence Chopin's compositional method.

When Chopin was twelve, it was decided that he should begin formal lessons with Józef Elsner, a composer, teacher, and director of the
Warsaw Conservatory. He also happened to be friends with Chopin's
father, Nicholas. Elsner suggested that Chopin read a book on theory
by Karol Antoni Simon, *Krótka nauka poznania Reguł Harmonii*. The
central chapters of the book are concerned with scales, keys, intervals,
chords, and particular rules for playing the "general bass." Elsner was a
successful and prolific composer in his own right, although he is best
known now as Chopin's teacher. Before meeting the young genius,
Elsner traveled around Europe, playing and conducting his pieces in
the latter years of the eighteenth century. By 1799, he settled in Warsaw and worked as part of the Polish National Theater, writing opera
and curating weekly concerts for the music-going public. Although he
was well versed in the Viennese School of classical music, writing eight
symphonies and numerous chamber pieces, Elsner was one of the first
composers to infuse his music with Polish national elements. He composed two Rondos "à la mazurek" and a Rondo à la krakowiak (Chopin
would also write one of these). He composed lots of operas, including
many on Polish libretti. His Polish operas were ahead of their time, and
he found an appreciative audience for them in Warsaw. It was probably
one of his biggest disappointments that he could not convince Chopin
to write a Polish opera. He founded the Society for Religious and National Music in 1814, reflecting his interest in religious music. He himself composed an enormous amount of religious works, among them
twenty-four Latin Masses, nine Polish Masses, and the passion-oratorio,
Męka Pana Naszego Jezusa Chrystusa. In addition to being an active
composer and also a writer, he contributed articles and reviews to various publications. He penned a treatise on setting the Polish language to
music and two books on singing. Elsner was very proud of his prized
pupil, and Poland was very proud of Elsner, bestowing the Order of St.
Stanisław upon him in 1823.

Chopin began formal studies in other non-musical subjects at the
Lyceum where his father taught, and also took some organ lessons with
Wilhelm Würfel. Würfel proved to be a useful contact when Chopin
made his first visit abroad to Vienna. His former organ teacher introduced the now nineteen-year-old Chopin (recent graduate of the Con-

servatory) to Carl Czerny, pianist and teacher of the famed Liszt, piano manufacturers Graf and Stein, and Tobias Haslinger, music publisher, among others.

Nothing could dampen Chopin's love of the piano, of course, not even some of the odd keyboard instruments available at the time. One of them, the pantaleon, was featured in one of his concerts in 1825. Invented in the last years of the seventeenth century by violinist and composer Pantaleon Hebenstreit (1668–1750), the pantaleon was already fading into obscurity by the nineteenth century. The piano's reign as the king of keyboard instruments was already established, especially with the artistry of Broadwood, Érard, and Pleyel behind it. Still, as a curiosity, the pantaleon was a novel choice, and Chopin improvised on the instrument to the delight of everyone.

At the age of nineteen, Chopin stood at a crossroads. He knew that leaving Warsaw long-term was his best chance at success, but figuring out how to do that was challenging. Would his future success lie in performance? In composition? In teaching? Or in a combination of those three things? He was clearly deeply committed to composition and more ambivalent about performance. This ambivalence probably urged him to think more seriously about teaching.

When he arrived in Paris, he came into contact with some important people in musical circles, including pianist and teacher Friedrich Kalkbrenner. Kalkbrenner was not universally loved or even respected. He was considered by some a pompous name-dropper. The brilliant pianist Clara Schumann thought he was full of himself, while Mendelssohn thought he was a plagiarist. Kalkbrenner, for his part, saw an opportunity in Chopin, and offered to become the young man's teacher for the subsequent three years. Chopin bowed to this man, whom he considered a technical talent, but ultimately declined the offer. Chopin was transitioning from student into teacher, satisfied with what he had learned thus far, ready to share his experiences with students.

Finding students, though, was difficult at the beginning. His debut concert in Paris was an artistic success but had a less than stellar financial outcome. His family sent money from Poland, hoping to keep him afloat until he found his feet under him. During this frantic search for performing opportunities and students, Paris was struck with a devastating cholera epidemic followed by politically motivated riots. What few students Chopin had were lost, as people of means fled the city. It was a chance encounter that supposedly turned the tide, although this story is probably more legend than fact. The story goes that Chopin ran into Prince Walenty Radziwiłł, who invited him to a party at the home of Baron James de Rothschild. There he was asked to play, and he impressed the baroness so much, she asked Chopin to teach her. In reality, Chopin likely just held on by his fingertips until the difficulty passed. Slowly, but surely, he built up a rather impressive collection of students. By his second year in Paris, Chopin was popular in both social circles and as a teacher. He was awed by his good fortune, stating, "I can't imagine what miracle is responsible for all this since I really haven't done anything to bring it about." Chopin's success as a teacher was due in no small part to his own work meeting and charming prospective students, but it was also a product of the very strong foundation he received from his teachers. Their work and Chopin's own philosophy made him one of the most sought-after teachers in Paris in the 1830s and 1840s.

LEARNING THROUGH ÉTUDES

When we think of typical piano lessons, we may think of scales and exercises to increase flexibility and strength. But a student cannot live on methods alone; the soul of every young musician cries out to play music that sounds like music, not just seemingly interminable repeating patterns. Études are musical pieces with ulterior motives. Many composers have written études: Johann Baptist Cramer, Johann Nepomuk Hummel, and of course, Muzio Clementi. A single étude may seek to work on a particular technique or issue. For Chopin, each étude brought some concept to musical life. It might have been a particular stretch or hand position. Chopin's preoccupation with the fingers and understanding their inherent strengths and weaknesses, for example, inspired many of these studies. Chopin's études not only represent a developing style of playing that reflects the new aspects of the piano, but they also provide an encapsulation of Chopin's unique style.

Chopin composed three sets, two of twelve (opps. 10 and 25) and one set of three, twenty-seven in total, all written within a decade from 1829 to 1839. A few of the popular études have acquired titles, although none of them were Chopin's invention. The first set of twelve was composed between 1829 and 1832, and published—revised and reordered—the following year. Chopin dedicated the set to Franz Liszt. The next set was composed between 1832 and 1836. This set was dedicated to Liszt's mistress, Marie d'Agoult, although no one is exactly certain why. The final three were written in 1839, and they were meant to be part of a piano pedagogy book by Ignaz Moscheles and François-Joseph Fétis called *Piano Playing School*. Moscheles, who met Chopin in Paris in 1839, asked for these études personally. Chopin, who had at first been critical of Moscheles, was won over by one of his colleague's pieces, and the two thereafter maintained a warm friendship.

Piano students all over the world are still assigned Chopin études, not only because they are carefully constructed pedagogical pieces, but also because, despite their technical aim, they are beautiful. In addition to becoming a standard tool of piano pedagogy, the études have also become concert pieces. Some individual études require mastery at a level unachievable by many players. To be able to play all of Chopin's twenty-seven études means being able to play just about anything in the established repertoire. Rather than analyze all of them, what follows are notes on some of the exemplary études composed by Chopin.

The first étude in the op. 10 collection (known to some as the "Waterfall") features musical passages that test the extension in the right hand and also ask the player to play arpeggiated chords along the entire range of the instrument. Chopin seems to be suggesting that in asking players to go over these distances (giving them specific fingerings, of course), they will discover that it makes more sense to pivot with the index finger and not the middle finger, as one might assume. A piece like this is designed not just to emphasize the strong physical aspects of the hand, but to de-emphasize the weak ones.

The third étude in the op. 10 set is less about fireworks and fast-moving notes, although it is by no means static. The pianist must address the issue of legato, of connectedness. The pianist must also deal with the proper way to play rubato, with flexibility in the rhythm. In his notes on the études, Alfred Cortot said this of the legato aspect of this piece: "The rubato tempo maintained throughout the Study must moreover never be either fitfully marked or exaggerated in any way. Indeed, it should follow faithfully the natural quickening or slowing of declamation which sometimes lingers though emotion, and at other times is sped on by eagerness."

Op. 10, no. 3 stands out from the rest of the set because of its cantabile quality. Some have read emotion into this quality, giving this étude the nickname "Farewell" ("L'Adieu") or "Sadness" ("Tristesse"). It evokes more than simply sadness, however. We might read into it a sense of wistfulness or nostalgia. There is an anecdote about this étude that involves Chopin becoming overwhelmed with emotion and exclaiming, "Oh, my homeland!" while playing this piece. Whatever the intended emotion, it is exceedingly beautiful. The form is ABA, like many études. The middle section changes character somewhat, for contrast—and Chopin's technical demands increase, but when the initial theme returns, it is even more achingly lovely.

In op. 10, no. 11 Chopin asks the pianist to roll chords: that is, to play all of the notes of a block chord in quick succession, creating the effect of a chord played on the strings of a harp. Along with these rolled chords comes a melody, and the person playing must be able to bring out this single melodic line out of these chords. The melody notes are often atop these chords, but there are moments when the melody notes appear as one of the inner notes. Being able to create a cohesive melody line in this case is the challenge. Keeping the speed of the rolled chords steady requires dexterity and control, two other aspects that need attention in this étude.

The final étude of the op. 10 is the so-called Revolutionary Étude. Of course, this was not Chopin's choice, but the name—and the sentiment it is associated with—has made this one of the composer's most recognizable works. It was composed in the autumn of 1831—Chopin's first year in Paris. Away from home as he was, and worried for his friends and family, he could only distill his great emotion into work. In his diary in September of that year, Chopin—mostly reticent in public about the political turmoil in Poland—gave voice to his own frustrations. Did God exist, and if so, how could He not avenge the Russian crimes against Poland? One can certainly read Chopin's frustration and anger in this work, whether or not he intended it. The piece begins with dramatic chord followed by a scurrying line downward. The left hand seemingly never stops moving, while the right hand plays a bold melody. It is a stormy and conflicted work, with a seemingly never-ending outpouring of emotion. Even the few instances that feel less stormy are still overwrought. It is no wonder this étude has become so well known.

In op. 25, the first étude is in A-flat and is known as the "Aeolian Harp." It requires the pianist to maintain a stream of notes in the melody and an active accompaniment. Once again, the pianist must find ways to bring the melody out of the lush texture. The second étude in the op. 25 set has a challenge not of melody but of time: keeping one hand maintaining eighth-note triplets (in pairs) and the left hand working against that with a single quarter-note triplet. It is uncommon to hear this piece referred to by a nickname, although the busy melody led someone to start calling it "Bees."

No. 5 in the set abounds with minor seconds, a small and dissonant interval. On first hearing, a listener may worry that the pianist is making some mistakes, leading to the moniker "Wrong Note." The left hand part includes large rolled chords. In the center section, which switches to the major mode, the left hand takes over the melody while the right plays a complex accompaniment with wide-spaced chords and arpeggios. The ending section draws on neither of the established themes, but rather ends with a declamatory rising arpeggio.

In nos. 6, 8, and 10, Chopin challenges the pianist to maintain running intervals. In no. 6, the right hand must play a barrage of thirds, quickly and accurately. In no. 8, Chopin gives parallel sixths to both hands. The composer was careful to specify the fingerings, and a student learning should pay close attention to them. No. 10 asks for chromatic octaves in both hands. There is no doubt that mastery of pieces like these brings dexterity, ease of motion, and superb control. In no. 10, there are also longer notes in the middle of the octaves that are meant to be held for longer values than the octaves around them. This is the biggest hurdle in this demanding piece, and it's one that many pianists skirt around by not holding these middle notes for their full value. The final étude in the op. 25 set, "Ocean," is a stormy and passionate journey up and down the keyboard for both hands. There is some controversy on how to interpret these lush chromatic chords. Which notes are to be emphasized? And how does one remain in control of these breaking waves while still having them feel natural and somewhat wild?

Chopin's final three études from 1839, the ones he composed for Moscheles, are less demanding than those from opp. 10 and 25. The first two seem primarily concerned with time issues, polyrhythms specifically. The third of the set challenges the player to keep two musical ideas in the right hand—a legato melody line on top and a choppier middle line. The independence of voices was so important to Chopin's method, and it's quite fitting that this was his final word in études. A performance of all three of this set without opus number will not last longer than seven minutes. Careful study of all of Chopin's twenty-seven études will strengthen more than just a pianist's hand strength and technical ability, but will also increase sensitivity, artistry, and expression—all qualities valued by the master.

2

CHOPIN'S CONCERT LIFE

It is August 11, 1829, and you are the illustrious new talent, Fryderyk Chopin. You are standing backstage at the Kärntnerthortheater waiting to make your debut on the concert stage in Vienna. You're nineteen years old, on your first trip to Vienna. In the hands of your organ teacher, Wilhelm Würfel, who convinced you to do this, you feel pretty confident. You've been playing for years in the homes of the rich and powerful in Warsaw, but this concert is your first foray onto the world stage. The experience fills you with more than a little anxiety, but you take the stage and are greeted by a warm ovation. The audience loves your music; they respond enthusiastically, and it's wonderful. You repeat the concert with a few changes a couple of days later to a similar reaction. A young man, you handle the stress of these concerts fairly well, and when you move to Paris in 1831, you're ready to take on the challenge of more public appearances. Your Paris debut is stellar, and it seems that you have found yourself at something of a crossroads: continue playing public concerts and touring, or focus your energies on teaching and composition. For a time, you try to do all of it.

As time goes by, however, and your body starts to succumb to illness more frequently, the exertion of performing becomes a burden you're not sure you want to bear. One of your friends in Paris is the famous pianist, Franz Liszt. You often perform with him on concerts, and you are constantly amazed by his ability to get in front of crowds—sometimes madly wild for him—and perform without a hint of worry. He seems to thrive on the energy of the people, coming to life on the stage.

You like smaller rooms, soirées with friends and new acquaintances. You like nothing more than to play into the wee hours with your fellow musicians where you can truly be yourself and where your sometimes delicate touch isn't criticized for not being loud enough. You decide, for the good of your physical and mental health, to choose the path of composing and teaching. Late in life, financial straits will call you again to travel to the stages of England and Scotland, but the experience will consume your precious energy when you have little to spare.

Chopin's journey from that exciting debut in Vienna in 1829 to the final concert in 1848 is the central focus of this chapter. We begin with the first concerts given by young Fryderyk Chopin, the musical prodigy. His parents chose not to push their son to perform too often, and in fact, his early public concert appearances were sparse. Private performances were more common, however, with Chopin a favorite entertainer of some of the aristocrats in Warsaw. As he matured, Chopin looked to a future living abroad. To this end, he composed two piano concertos as showpieces for his talent. In addition to a discussion of these works, we also touch upon a couple of the other orchestral pieces Chopin composed for these important performances. His early success was helped along by the attention of critics, especially Robert Schumann, who was a fellow composer and pianist. We spend a little time getting to know Schumann and his unique contribution to Chopin's burgeoning career. The chapter comes to a close with a recounting of Chopin's later performances and his final tour to England and Scotland.

EARLY CONCERT LIFE

As a young boy, Wolfgang Mozart toured around with his father and sister (also a talented young musician), impressing the aristocracy with his skills at so tender an age. Beethoven's father, knowing that genius looks better the younger you are, lied about his son's age when advertising his concerts. Child prodigies are fascinating creatures. There is something compelling about the special promise of a youngster who displays talent far beyond his or her years. When he was seven years old, Chopin began composing. His Polonaise in B-flat major was copied down by Mikołaj Chopin, Fryderyk's father, followed by the Polonaise in G minor and a couple of marches and a set of variations that were subsequently lost. The *Warsaw Press* ran a story about this young musical genius, noting that Poland had indeed produced a prodigy, who could not only play virtuosic pieces on the piano, but write astounding music of his own.

Once the word was out, it was time for a public appearance. Countess Zofia Zamoyska hatched the idea of featuring young Chopin in a concert to benefit victims of the Napoleonic Wars. An announcement in a local paper said, in part:

> A vocal and instrumental concert for the benefit of the poor will take place in the theater of the Radziwiłł Palace, given by the best-known musicians of this capital as well as some newly arrived artists. . . . Music, which touches our spirits with its tender melodies . . . cannot help but contribute to the relief of human suffering.

Chopin's teacher, Wojciech Żywny, who was Czech, chose the music of another Czech composer for Chopin's big debut. Young Fryderyk played the Piano Concerto in E minor by Adalbert Gyrowetz (Jírovec). Soon, all of the aristocrats in Poland wanted the young man to come visit. The Grand Duke Constantine Pavlovitch, brother of the tsar and a strange man who acted by turns cruel and despondent, enjoyed listening to young Fryderyk play. Also fans of the genius: Prince Sapieha, Count Potocki, Prince and Princess Czartoryski, and of course, Countess Zamoyska.

Although his first public concert went well, Justyna and Mikołaj did not allow their son to play another public concert for five years. Perhaps they did not want to disrupt their routines or neglect the needs of their other children. In contrast to their caution, we look at another piano prodigy, Franz Liszt. When Liszt was just nine years old, he made his first public appearance in Öldenburg, and before he was a teenager, he played more public concerts than Chopin would in his entire life. Rather than parading him out for the general public, the Chopins allowed young Fryderyk to play privately for some members of the upper class. Notable among Chopin's visits to the aristocracy was his audience with Maria Feodorovna, the mother of the tsar, to whom young Chopin presented two Polish dances. The private performance took place in the Warsaw Lyceum, where Mikołaj Chopin was a teacher. Although Mikołaj had had a political past, he had no desire to involve his son in revolutionary politics.

Chopin's second public concert took place in Warsaw in February of 1823. He was just about to turn thirteen. The performance was for another benefit concert, this time for the Warsaw Charitable Society. Chopin's featured work for the concert was a piano concerto by Ferdinand Ries, who had studied with Beethoven. A review of the concert review spoke glowingly of Chopin's talent, which "aroused everyone's admiration." It went on to say, "We can confidently say that we have not heard a virtuoso to date in our capital who could overcome such astonishing difficulties with so much ease and accuracy." The review also talks about another young man making waves in Vienna, a one Mr. Franz Liszt (whose name they misspelled as "List"), but makes it clear that "our capital possesses certainly his equal if not his superior in the person of . . . young M. Chopin."

On his first trip abroad five years later in 1829, Chopin went to Vienna, where his former organ teacher Wilhelm Würfel introduced him to a publisher, a theater director, and other pianists. They insisted Chopin play a concert, which he did on August 11. The venue was the Kärntnerthortheater, which had been the location of the premiere of Beethoven's Ninth Symphony five years earlier. The program consisted of established works like the Overture to Beethoven's only ballet, *The Creatures of Prometheus*; an aria from a Rossini opera; and a rondo and chorus from an opera by Nicola Vaccaj. Interspersed with these pieces were two improvisations from Chopin, one on a Mozart theme (presumably "La ci darem la mano" from *Don Giovanni*) and the other on a theme from a contemporary opera, *La Dame Blanche* by Boïeldieu. The latter was so enthusiastically received, he was sent back out on stage to improvise on something else. He chose the lively Polish folk song, "Chmiel," often heard at weddings. Chopin's improvisations of this raucous drinking song impressed everyone. In a letter to his family, Chopin explained that this work in particular excited the audience "as they are not used here to such songs. My spies in the stalls assure me that people even jumped on the seats." By all accounts, the audience went wild for Chopin's talent, cheering on their feet for this young man. The only criticism was that he played too quietly.

Chopin gained more than a few fans of great importance. Among them were Count Moritz Dietrichstein, friend of the emperor; Count Moritz Lichnowsky (brother of Prince Karl, who was an important patron of Beethoven); and Count Wenzel Robert Gallenberg, owner of the Kärntnerthortheater, who stood to make a great deal more money off young Mr. Chopin. Under pressure from these gentlemen to repeat his success, Chopin agreed to a second concert a week after the first.

One of the notable performances from these performances was the *Rondo à la Krakowiak*. At eighteen years old, Chopin composed the piece under the careful supervision of Elsner. It very much impressed and intrigued the Viennese audience. The *krakowiak* is a traditional Polish dance in duple meter usually danced by couples. It was a popular folk dance, but it had also transitioned into fashionable high society. In the stylized versions of it, there are three sections; the two outer sections are similar, and a contrasting section resides in the center. Chopin constructed his piece as a rondo, suggesting that there is a melody or theme that returns over and over again. That recurring theme is a *krakowiak* melody. Chopin brings out the spirited rhythm of the style, which relies heavily on syncopated rhythms, and allows the soloist to shine in a skilled display of pianistic dexterity. It starts with a stately introduction. The low instruments lay down a bed of sound, over which the soloist plays a theme in a somewhat free manner. Then the fireworks begin. The pianist plays a virtuosic passage followed by the rhythmic entrance of the orchestra and the pianist. Throughout, the orchestra plays a supportive and accompanimental role for the most part. Chopin shows skill in writing for the ensemble, and he is very sensitive to the strengths of each instrument, even though the soloist is the star.

At the second concert, the audience was larger and incredibly appreciative. The reviews were favorable again, although there was some mixed opinion about the rondo. Of course, the press in Vienna emphasized Würfel's influence on the young talent: "The master displayed his ability as a pianist of the highest order and successfully surmounted the most enormous difficulties. . . . This young man, who is reported to owe his early training to Herr Würfel, displays a serious attempt to weave the orchestra and piano parts of his compositions together in an interesting style." The day after this second concert, Chopin was on his way back to Poland. The trip had been an artistic success, but not a financial one. The contacts he made in Vienna were certainly appreciative of his talent, but many had ulterior motives of making a profit off the talents of the naïve youngster. Chopin went back to Poland no richer, but a bit more well known.

Chopin passed through Prague on the way back to Poland. He was asked to give a concert, but refused, claiming a lack of time. The true reason was the fickle public, which had given the virtuoso Niccolò Paganini a tepid reception. Chopin stopped briefly in Teplice, where he played privately for Prince Clary-Aldringen, and Dresden, finally arriving in Warsaw about three weeks from his departure from Vienna. Suddenly Warsaw seemed a bit claustrophobic, and Chopin was soon planning future adventures.

The musical season at the local businessman's club, the Resursa, offered some diversion. Chopin may have brought his Variations on Mozart's "La ci darem la mano" to the stage. He also sat in the audience for a number of concerts, including an operetta called *The Millionaire Peasant*, which was composed by a friend, Józef Damse. A song from the operetta "Brooms" ("Miotelki") stuck with Chopin, and he played variations on it at the Resursa that December. He also played for some singers. Chopin's appearance was valued highly by the Polish audience, but in truth, the composer was just biding his time for the next opportunity to travel. In preparation, he was working on a couple of works for orchestra.

PIANO CONCERTOS I AND 2

At nineteen years old, Fryderyk Chopin was finishing up his formal education at the Warsaw Conservatory. In considering opportunities to perform abroad, Chopin understood that one of the best things to bring with him was a piano concerto. The piano concerto as a genre had decades of history before Chopin put his hand to it. Wolfgang Amadeus Mozart was as talented a pianist as he was a composer, and he used piano concertos to raise his profile when he moved to Vienna. He wrote more than two dozen in total over the course of his life, and within that time, brought a level of artistry to the genre that would carry it into the next century. As the Romantic period began to take shape, it was clear that the composer-virtuoso would take the piano concerto and bring it to the next level. Beethoven was part of this (with his five piano concertos), as were Chopin and Robert Schumann. Later Romantic composers like Liszt and Sergei Rachmaninoff pushed the limits of virtuosity with their piano concertos. It remains a viable genre even today, although there are very few virtuosos who are also composers.

Chopin stood at an interesting place. For him, the piano concerto was a three-movement work, with quick first and last movements, and a slower central movement. The established form of the first movement was usually an Allegro with two themes, presented first by the orchestra and then by the piano soloist. Within that first movement, there would also be a solo passage called a cadenza. During the cadenza, which might have been improvised by the soloist or meticulously planned out and written down, the orchestra is entirely silent, waiting for their cue to come back in and play. When Mozart composed some of his concertos he was the intended soloist, so he may have just initially left his part sketched out or absent altogether for the premiere. Cadenzas were sometimes written down later in preparation for publication. Sometimes composers provided cadenzas for earlier piano concertos written by others. Beethoven, for example, wrote cadenzas for Mozart's Piano Concerto No. 20. German composer Wilhelm Kempff (1895–1991) wrote out cadenzas for Beethoven's Piano Concertos Nos. 1–4.

Unlike other Romantic composers like Liszt or even Beethoven, Chopin had no great desire to reinvent the concerto form. Chopin's Piano Concertos show a conservative style in the orchestral writing, but where they are truly unique and special is in the music for the soloist. The melodic material that is first presented by the orchestra is lovely, but in the hands of the soloist, it is magic. Chopin truly succeeded—and certainly this was his foremost intention—in creating stunning showpieces for himself. The orchestra in Chopin's concertos supports and encourages. It does not overpower. It stays in the background most of the time, but it shapes the harmonies that highlight Chopin's delightful melodies.

Chopin intended to use some Polish forms in his first Piano Concerto, as the Polish-influenced music he'd already played in other parts of Europe seemed to be among the most popular. On his first trip to Vienna in 1829, he impressed the crowd with improvised variations on the Polish folk song "Chmiel," and his sprightly *Rondo à la Krakowiak*. These adaptations of folk music sounded fresh to the ears of the Viennese public, and Chopin understood that the novelty of this music could both boost his popularity and help him distinguish himself from other up-and-coming talents.

Chopin also had an innate understanding of the piano, its strengths and weaknesses and its potential, but he felt less sure in working with the instruments of the orchestra, many of which he had not likely played. Having a difficult time with the orchestra's part, at the beginning of 1830, he gathered some musicians for a private run through at his parents' place. A critic invited to be among the small audience wrote for the *Gazeta Polska* that the piece was lovely, but Chopin remained unsatisfied. He spent February of 1830 working on it. The piece he finally completed in 1830 came to be known as the Piano Concerto No. 2 in F minor. The following year, Chopin completed another piano concerto, this one ultimately called the Piano Concerto No. 1 in E minor. (The reversed numbering reflects the order of publication.)

In March of 1830, Chopin performed the Piano Concerto No. 2 in F minor at the Polish National Theater in Warsaw. It was extremely well received, and the entire concert was repeated—with small changes— less than a week later. The Polish public was immediately smitten with Chopin's charming use of national dance rhythms and folksongs. In October of that same year, Chopin presented one final concert in War- saw, this one featuring the E minor Concerto. After the success of this concert—which was not quite as overwhelming as the one in March— Chopin finally left for Vienna, where he spent eight months. He was not able to repeat the success he'd had there previously, and he moved on to Paris with the intention of going to London, but he ended up making Paris his home thereafter.

There are three movements in Piano Concerto No. 1 in E minor. The first movement, marked Allegro maestoso, is as majestic as its marking suggests. The orchestral exposition seems to hold itself back a little, but once the piano enters, the movement opens up and shows its noble bearing. The second movement, marked Romanze Larghetto, is a nocturne that virtually sings with tunefulness. A nocturne is simply a musical piece that evokes the night. Chopin is probably the best-known composer of solo piano nocturnes, a genre that is thoroughly Romantic. (He wrote twenty-one of them.) There is no conflict here, no over- wrought drama. Chopin's gift for melody absolutely shines. At the end of the movement, lovely bassoon lines intertwine with the piano, giving us a chance to distinctly hear the woodwinds and piano together. The music of Poland appears in the finale, a Rondo – vivace that features Chopin's take on the effervescent *krakowiak*, a dance—as its name suggests—originating in the southern area near Kraków. Chopin paid homage to his homeland in numerous pieces, both big and small, and here he brings this lively dance to an international audience.

The opening movement of the F minor Concerto, marked Maestoso, is sufficiently dramatic, with the piano soloist taking on most of the thematic development. In this movement, Chopin eschews the traditional cadenza, possibly because the entire movement has had the soloist as its focal point. The second movement seems to draw upon the *bel canto* style popular in the Italian operas of the time. The piano part may seem improvisational, but it was meticulously planned. The delicacy and intimacy of the movement come more sharply into focus when we realize that while writing this piece, Chopin claimed to have been thinking of a young woman he'd known (and loved) at the Warsaw Conservatory. The final movement, an Allegro vivace, was inspired by the mazurka, another Polish dance. The piano again gets the spotlight, with the orchestra providing accents and punctuation. The soloist never rests, and indeed the virtuosity, ornamentation, and adventurous lines continue to the very end of this scintillating rondo.

Although Chopin included Polish folk music in his works to exploit the "exotic" tastes of the Viennese and Parisians, there are also political implications of Chopin's use of folk music. Chopin, because he had emigrated, was able to give voice to a culture oppressed by the tsar. Certainly Chopin wrote in this manner because he missed his homeland, but there is a definite sense that he felt the need to show the larger musical world the beauty of Polish folk music, a tradition that was surely being crushed under political machinery (see chapter 5).

As the remainder of Chopin's output would prove, the two piano concertos are something of an anomaly in a key respect: Chopin wrote just a handful of orchestral pieces. Chopin composed the Fantasia on Polish Airs in 1828 when he was eighteen, although its premiere didn't come until two years later. Chopin presented this piece at his first large-scale concert at the National Theater in Warsaw in March of 1830. It features two national song styles of Poland and a Polish folk song that was favored by Chopin's mother. The Fantasia begins with a slow introduction, marked *Largo ma non troppo*, that is almost nocturne-like in character. Chopin then presents the three tunes and follows with variations for each. The first theme is the popular song, "Już miesiac zeszedł," or "The Moon Has Set." The second theme is a brooding minor-mode melody written by opera composer Karol Kurpiński, who used the form of a Ukranian dance called the *dumka* (this melody was taken from Kurpiński's larger work, *Elegy on the Death of Tadeusz Kościuszko*). The third theme is a buoyant *kujawiak*, the perfect antipode to the elegiac middle section. This quick final section features brilliant passagework that brings the work to an energetic close.

Chopin began composing the Grand Polonaise in E-flat major for piano and orchestra in 1830. He completed the main section of it in 1831, but then added a solo piano piece to act as an introduction. The introduction, marked *Andante spianato*, was written a few years after the Polonaise, and Chopin planned to show great contrast between these sections. The opening part is docile and calm, almost suggesting some of the gentler and evocative pieces in Chopin's solo piano repertoire. The sinuous right hand melody and the flowing accompaniment lull the listener into a peaceful state of mind. Horn calls then introduce both the Polonaise and a change of mood.

The orchestral opening of the Polonaise itself is noble, yet delicate. The piano enters, and the orchestra provides colorful accents and a sense of great warmth. The piano part is surely challenging, with quick scalar passages and thick harmonies. One can imagine how impressive and self-assured this piece must have sounded to audiences. The designation *brillante* is perfectly apt here, as the playing of the soloist is scintillating. He might not have known it at the time, but this would be Chopin's last work for the orchestra, and it is a fitting farewell, indeed.

ROBERT SCHUMANN

As a young composer in Paris, Chopin's success depended on many factors. Publicity, then as now, was a crucial thing for up-and-coming talent. Although Chopin's concert performances were mostly well received, he disliked the pressure and disruption caused by public performances and preferred to play for smaller, more intimate gatherings of friends. In the absence of publicity for public performances, reviews of music became an even more important source of press. One of the voices speaking about Chopin when he arrived in Paris was Ludwig Rellstab, a composer and a critic from Berlin whose conservative tastes were at odds with the flowering of Romanticism. In the periodical he founded in 1830, *Iris im Geliebte der Tonkunst*, he claimed that Chopin had "vandalized" Mozart's "La ci darem la mano" melody for his variations. He was also critical of Chopin's op. 11 Piano Concerto. Later, in an 1833 review of Chopin's mazurkas, Rellstab complained of "ear-splitting dissonances" and "grating modulations." Chopin needed balancing voices in the press, journalists and critics to champion his works. One notable voice belonged to a fellow composer.

In addition to being a gifted composer, Robert Schumann was also a music journalist (1810–1856). He was born in the same year as Chopin, and outlived him by only seven years. He, along with Friedrich Wieck (his future father-in-law) and Ludwig Schuncke, founded *Neue Zeitschrift für Musik* (*NZfM*) in 1834. In the Romantic spirit of the time, these men decided to begin a journal to discuss art and music and champion the creation of both. It took months to get the project off the ground, and there were challenges both in the practical realm—finding a publisher—and in the philosophical—figuring out the purpose and mission of the journal. Schumann himself did not intend to write reviews, but rather more general essays about music as an art. However, when contributors could not be found, Schumann took on that role, and indeed, many of those reviews have become important first-person accounts of emerging talent.

His very first review of a musical piece was written when he was twenty-one years old, and it appeared not in the *NZfM*, but in another journal called the *Allgemeine musikalische Zeitung*. It was a review of Chopin's Variations on Mozart's "La ci darem la mano" from *Don Giovanni*. It is not a straightforward review, however. Schumann was interested in both music and literature, and in his work, the two often intersected. For his review of Chopin's work, Schumann created something of a narrative story, with characters. One character in his story was Julius Knorr, a real person. The other two were invented: Florestan and Eusebius. Schumann would later add a third character named Raro in articles he wrote for *Der Komet*, and in these articles he would declare that all three men were part of a music society called the *Davidsbündler* (League of David). The purpose of the society was to defend the cause of new music, and "swat the Philistines musical and otherwise" who wanted only the comfortable status quo. The reference to David and the Philistines obviously draws on the Biblical story of the warrior David, who triumphed over Goliath, and is credited with writing many of

the Psalms. The *Davidsbündler* articles are written as narratives, almost
as if they are excerpts from a novel, which it seems they were intended
to be.

Florestan, Eusebius, and Raro are literary devices, meant to portray
differing temperaments and opinions, all the better to convey discussions about music, art, and creativity. Florestan is impetuous, quick, and
passionate; Eusebius is gentle, orderly, and cautious; Raro is methodical
and rational. Some reviews have sections "authored" by each of these
characters, and sometimes there is dialogue. Schumann might include
an analysis of the music that is unsigned by any of the characters. Schumann characterized them in many comments: "Florestan is, as you
know, one of those peculiar musical individuals who seems to anticipate
long in advance anything innovatory, new or unusual." He is quick to
understand and quick to boredom, while Eusebius, on the other hand,
"comprehends with more difficulty, but more surely." As players, Florestan shows the greater fireworks at the keyboard, but Eusebius the
greater technical ability and deeper intellectual connection.

In his review of the Variations by Chopin, Florestan enters the
room—Chopin's Variations in his hands—and utters the oft-quoted bit
about Chopin: "Hats off, gentlemen—a genius." Eusebius then plays
the piece at the piano. Florestan has fallen asleep on Julius Knorr,
editor-in-chief of the *NZfM*. In listening, the review states that "genius
is evident in every measure" and goes on to describe what the characters must be doing in each variation, creating a story to go with the
music that matches up with actions in the opera. Another favorable
review was written by Friedrich Wieck, but Chopin did not appreciate
either review, and in fact actively disliked Wieck's. Wieck gave the
piece to his daughter, Clara, who was embarking on a career as a piano
virtuoso. It thereafter became a standard piece in her repertoire, although it was a challenge at first. In her diary, she declared it "the
hardest piece I have ever seen or played till now." Even though she was
only twelve years old at the time, the piece took her just eight days to
learn.

Robert Schumann met Chopin in Leipzig in September of 1835,
when both men were twenty-five. They saw each other again a year
later in the same city. Schumann wrote to Chopin a few times, but
Chopin seems to have ignored most of Schumann's attempts at familiar-
ity. Robert Schumann was the dedicatee of Chopin's Ballade No. 2, and

Chopin was the dedicatee of Schumann's *Kreisleriana* (op. 16). Schumann further paid homage to his contemporary by writing Variations on one of Chopin's nocturnes (G minor, op. 15 no. 3). In his collection of piano miniatures, *Carnaval*—an imagined masked ball—Schumann includes a piece called "Chopin." Also "invited" to *Carnaval* were "Florestan," "Eusebius," "Paganini," and "Chiarina" (for Clara).

There were numerous pianist-composers in Paris in the 1830s, and it's quite something that Chopin so impressed Schumann. Schumann knew the Mozart Variations intimately (having played them) and saw brilliance in their design. Chopin also chose an older piece as the source material for his Variations, which set him apart from those writing variations on contemporary opera themes from the works of Donizetti and Bellini. As Schumann scholar Leon Plantinga notes, "The difference between Chopin's variations and the common run of compositions of its kind is a subtle one; but Schumann saw it clearly."

Schumann was a champion of new music, and as a composer himself, saw the challenges facing those attempting to write innovative and provocative works. Critics seemed ready to tear down new music, leaving it unprogrammed on concerts and unheard. Schumann must have believed that as a creator and a critic, he stood in a unique and important position to make things better for the creators. In discussing a critic's unfavorable review of Chopin's Variations, Florestan compares the art of a creative person to the work of a critic: "What is a whole volume of a journal in the face of a Chopin concerto? What is the pedant's lunacy compared to poetic frenzy?"

After the favorable review of the Mozart Variations, Schumann stayed mum on the subject of Chopin for a while. There are a few passing references here and there, but nothing of substance until 1836, when Schumann published an essay discussing Chopin's two piano concertos. Schumann felt the need to explain the absence of the up-and-coming composer in the pages of the journal and does so by having Eusebius say, essentially, that he was worried he wouldn't be able to find the right words to describe something so special to him. Eusebius also observed that Chopin was reaching for some new direction, and he wanted to wait for a while before commenting on it. What seems to be missing from Schumann's review of the piano concertos is an actual review and analysis of the pieces. Rather Schumann's article—at its heart—is a brief discussion of Chopin as a nationalist composer.

In Schumann's other writings about Chopin that exist from 1836 through 1842, there is a good deal of positive feedback, although one will likely glean that Schumann was disappointed that there was not more significant development or innovation. In fact, he said more than once that Chopin's work was instantly recognizable because it was all so similar. He acknowledged Chopin's original showing as fabulous, and worried that it was too much for him to be more than that. "When he has given you a whole succession of the rarest creations, and you understand him more easily, do you suddenly demand something different? This is like chopping down your pomegranate tree because it produces, year after year, nothing but pomegranates." And furthermore: "We fear he will never achieve a level higher than that he has already reached. . . . With his abilities he could have achieved far more, influencing the progress of our art as a whole."

In his 1841 review of Chopin's Sonata in B-flat minor in particular, Schumann did not seem to be happy with his fellow composer's progress. Although he talks about the abundance of beauty in the work, he also says that the choice of "sonata" as a title must be in jest: "[Chopin] seems to have taken four of his most unruly children and put them together, possibly thinking to smuggle them, as a sonata, into company where they might not be considered individually presentable." To Schumann it seemed that Chopin had lost his way, and gotten too wrapped up in virtuosity for its own sake. He decries "obstacles on almost every page" with indecipherable progressions. The second movement—again claiming the marking "Scherzo" was in name alone—he describes as a "funeral march with something even repulsive about it." Chopin for his part seemed neither pleased with Schumann's good reviews nor upset about the less positive ones. Despite the things they had in common, Chopin appears to have had little appreciation for Schumann as a composer. Nor did Chopin feel the same tug as Schumann did to support fellow composers. Although correspondence between them may have existed, it did not survive to the present day. All we have are Schumann's words (in reviews and his own personal diary entries) on one side and Chopin's chilly silence on the other.

LATER CONCERT LIFE

Chopin made his public debut in Paris on February 26, 1832, about five months after he began living in the city. He shared the program at the Salle Pleyel with twelve other people and performed three times on the program. He played his own Concerto No. 2, and then joined a quintet of pianists for Kalkbrenner's Grand Polonaise for six pianos (Kalkbrenner was one of the six). Finally, Chopin played a set of solo pieces including nocturnes and mazurkas, and of course his Variations on Mozart's "La ci darem la mano." The concert was well received, although criticism that Chopin's playing as too quiet—heard first in the review for his Viennese debut—was again repeated. François-Joseph Fétis wrote a review of the performance which made reference to this delicate quality, saying that Chopin's playing did not "carry sufficiently." But Fétis's review also praised Chopin as a true original: "Here is a young man who gives himself up to his innate impulses and, taking no-one as a model, has discovered, if not an utter renewal of piano music, at least a fragment of that which for so long has been sought in vain, namely an abundance of original ideas, the origins of which can nowhere be indicated." The new connections and publicity helped Chopin's career as a teacher, which would become his steadiest source of income.

In May of 1832, Chopin gave a public performance as part of a benefit concert given by Prince de la Moskowa. Again, Chopin performed the Concerto No. 2, but its reception was a little colder. A critic for *Le Temps* lamented that Chopin did not seem to know how to express original ideas in an orchestral setting. And once again, Chopin was noted as playing with a "limited power of sound." Chopin took most criticism very harshly, and there must have been a moment when he wondered if playing concerts was worth the publicity. But then, he also had to contend with the criticism of his written music by the likes of Ludwig Rellstab.

In March and April of 1833, Chopin performed pieces in concerts given by friends. In a concert given by Ferdinand Hiller, Chopin joined with Hiller and Liszt to perform a single movement from a concerto for three harpsichords by J. S. Bach. At a benefit for Harriet Smithson (who would marry composer Hector Berlioz in October of that year), he and Liszt played a four-hand sonata by George Onslow. There was another benefit for Smithson in 1834, and Chopin took part in that concert as well. On Christmas of that year, Chopin performed a concert organized by François Stoepel, critic and writer for the *Gazette Musicale de Paris.* Chopin and Liszt performed a couple of works together, including Ignaz Moscheles's Sonata in E-flat major for four hands and Liszt's *Grand Duo* on a theme by Mendelssohn for two pianos, four hands.

The year 1835 brought more opportunity to perform publicly, although Chopin remained quite selective. In early April, Chopin helped organize a benefit concert to help Polish orphans. He and Liszt performed along with a few others, and the effort raised five thousand francs for the cause. Unfortunately, though, the event proved to be something of a turning point for Chopin. Later—years after Chopin's death—Fétis wrote about the poor response the composer received that evening: "he garnered barely a few bravos from his most devoted friends." Wojciech Sowiński wrote that Chopin was so distressed by the experience that he decided to leave public performance behind. His final public performance—for many years, at least—took place at the end of April, 1835. It was a benefit concert held at the Paris Conservatoire. Chopin performed the Polonaise in E-flat major with an orchestra. Thereafter, he would play for only intimate friends or at gatherings attended by people he knew and liked. Chopin biographer Friedrich Niecks recounted the composer's thoughts about public performance in a conversation Chopin had with Liszt: "I am not suited to public appearances—the auditorium saps my courage, I suffocate in the exhalation of the crowd, I am paralyzed by curious glances, and the sight of strange faces compels me to silence." Chopin would remain publicly silent for the next dozen years.

He played his last public concert in Paris on February 16, 1848, sixteen years—almost to the day—after his debut. By then his health was precarious at best, with complications from the tuberculosis appearing more and more often. On this particular occasion he was also inconveniently suffering the flu, which was going around the city. Still, leading up to the event, Chopin seemed to be anticipating it without anxiety. He wrote to his sister Ludwika that all tickets had sold out: "I shall have the fashionable world of Paris." And that he did. The concert was a sensation, and Chopin performed beautifully. On the concert program there was a Mozart trio (with cellist Auguste Franchomme and violinist Jean-Delphin Alard), a nocturne, a Barcarole (op. 60), an

étude, some preludes, a few mazurkas, a waltz, and—with Franchomme—three movements of the Sonata in G minor. The audience,
made up of royalty, aristocrats, and a who's who of the Parisian music
scene, was quite enchanted with the show.

The Revolution of 1848 began in Paris less than a week later, and the
"fashionable world of Paris" was thrown into considerable disarray. Students had other things on their minds besides piano lessons, and the
aristocracy took shelter outside of the city. Chopin hadn't been composing much in the months leading up to the concert, so he had no new
works to sell. The only way to make money was to leave the city, so
Chopin accepted an offer to play some concerts in England and Scotland. Jane Stirling, a former student, took care of all of the details of
what would be Chopin's final performances. He spent seven months
abroad, playing small salons and recitals for, among others, Lady Gains-
borough, Marquis W. A. Douglas, the Duke of Sutherland, Lord Fal-
mouth, and Queen Victoria and Prince Albert. He also gave larger
concerts at Manchester's Concert Hall, Edinburgh's Hopetown Room,
and Glasgow's Merchant Hall. His very last performance took place in
London, at the Guild Hall. It was a charity event: the Polish Concert
and Ball. Due to some shortsighted programming choices, Chopin was
asked to play after some lively dancing, and the audience was not in a
state to listen to the kind of sensitive playing Chopin offered. It was,
very simply put, the wrong venue for his work. After it was over, Chopin
wrote to Stanisław Koźmian, "I have ended my public career." So it was.
Chopin returned to Paris soon after, his health very poor. It was November of 1848. The next year would be his last.

3

CONFIDANTS AND COLLABORATORS

Chopin enjoyed many friendships of varying depth throughout his life. Although his social circle was wide, he let himself be truly known only by very few. This chapter explores some of these close relationships, and the friends with whom Chopin lived and worked. The focus here will be on friendship and collaboration, leaving romantic entanglements for chapter 6. We begin with the friends Chopin made as a young man, most of whom were boarders in the Chopin home. After Chopin's arrival in Paris, he made the acquaintance of a young French cellist named Auguste Franchomme. Franchomme would become an important friend and collaborator, and indeed, some of the works Chopin composed for his friend (or with, in the case of the *Grand Duo Concertant sur des Thèmes de Robert le Diable*) form the musical heart of this chapter. Finally, we examine Chopin's relationship with the larger-than-life pianist and composer Franz Liszt.

BOYHOOD FRIENDS

Mikołaj and Justyna Chopin's home put a roof over the heads of their four children, Fryderyk, Ludwika, Emilia, and Izabela, until Emilia succumbed to tuberculosis in the spring of 1827. The family moved to a larger place after that tragic event, and took in a few boarders—students at the Lyceum, some of whom made lasting friendships with Fryderyk. Of the four most important, I mention three here: Jan

Białobłocki, Jan Matuszyński, and Julian Fontana (Tytus Wojciechowski will appear later). Chopin was destined to have the shortest friendship with Białobłocki, not because of conflict or strife, but because of Białobłocki's death at the age of twenty-two. After Białobłocki went off to study law at Warsaw University, he and Chopin corresponded, and thirteen of the composer's letters to Białobłocki survive. Mostly they deal with day-to-day activities, gossip about their mutual friends and acquaintances, and funny things that happened. But Białobłocki's health was precarious, and Chopin makes reference to this in the sincerest parts of his letters: "Give me a kiss, My Life. I wish nothing for you but recovery." In 1826, Chopin sent his friend some music to play, specifically piano solos of the music of Rossini, transcribed by Diabelli, a Polonaise of Kaczkowski, and some of Chopin's own "scrawls." The Polonaise, in particular, was meant to bring joy but also give something Białobłocki to play that would "exercise [his] fingers, which have doubtless gone stiff, if I may say so."

When the Chopins heard false rumors of Białobłocki's death, young Fryderyk rejoiced at finding out they was untrue. Revealing his dark sense of humor, Chopin wrote to his friend in March of 1827 in reference to the frightening news they had heard: "So, having dried my tear-swollen eyelids, I take up my pen to inquire of you, are you alive or did you die? If you are dead, please let me know, and I will tell the cook, for ever since she heard about it she has been saying her prayers." In that same letter, Chopin shifts moods quickly to let Białobłocki know that his sister Emilia had taken ill and been in bed for four weeks. Indeed, she would pass away less than a fortnight later. Białobłocki himself would last another year before dying, still a bachelor, at his family's estate.

Jan Matuszyński, whom Chopin called Jaś, would become Chopin's roommate in the mid-1830s. Chopin had rented an apartment (previously occupied by a friend of his) where he lived with Dr. Aleksander Hoffman. Hoffmann offered a calm balance to Chopin's sometimes anxious personality, and was there to give gentle medical advice to Chopin, whose health was often unsteady. The two lived together for two years, and when Hoffmann left, Chopin's old friend Jaś became his next roommate. Fortunately, Matuszyński was also a physician. The pair enjoyed living together, socializing with Chopin's new friends, and absorbing the culture of their adopted city. They even vacationed together. Chopin was particularly gratified to have someone with whom he could speak his native tongue, and also reaped the benefits of his friend's medical training. In 1835, Chopin returned to Paris after some travel abroad, and quickly succumbed to what was probably pneumonia. Luckily, Jaś was there to nurse Chopin through the first serious health crisis of his adulthood. Matuszyński earned a second doctorate while in Paris and eventually married Caroline Clothilde Boquet. Jaś and Chopin's cohabitation in what the composer referred to as a "gentleman's grotto" or "lion's lair" ended as Matuszyński got ready for his wedding and Chopin moved to a new apartment down the street.

Just a few short years later, Matuszyński's health began to decline due to tuberculosis. When he died, in April of 1842, just thirty-two years old, Chopin was with him. Accounts say that Matuszyński died in Chopin's arms. It was a difficult time, but Chopin was determined to stay strong as he watched his friend struggle with his final illness. Chopin's companion, George Sand, said at the time that Chopin only let himself fall apart after Jaś died. He was quite inconsolable for a time. Four years later, Chopin mentioned dear Jaś in a letter to his family: "There is not a day that I do not think of him."

Chopin had the longest and most involved relationship with Julian Fontana. Fontana did a fair bit of traveling in his adult life; after participating in the November Uprising, he moved to Hamburg, then to Paris, England, Paris again, Cuba, the United States, and Paris for the final fifteen years of his life. Chopin and Fontana connected on that first visit to Paris in 1832. On his second time there, which lasted for nine years, he began working with Chopin as a copyist. He also acted as the point of contact between the composer and his publishers. From what we can gather, Chopin never paid him for the work he did; however, Fontana was the dedicatee of the two Polonaises in op. 40.

In addition to duties pertaining to Chopin's music, Fontana was called upon to be something of a caretaker for Chopin's affairs when the composer traveled to Mallorca with George Sand. In December of 1838, Chopin instructed Fontana to pay his rent and give the porter at his building a New Year's gift of twenty francs. He also asked that Fontana be discreet about his ongoing illness, especially when talking to his banker friend, Léo, who often lent Chopin money, interest-free. In early 1839, a letter from Chopin begins:

> I send you the Preludes. Copy them, you and Wolff; I think there are
> no errors. Give the copy to Probst [Pröbst-Kistner publishers], and
> the manuscript to Pleyel. Take Probst's money, for which I enclose a
> note and *reçu*, at once to Léo; I have no time to write him a letter of
> thanks; and from the money that Pleyel will give you, that is: fifteen
> hundred francs, you can pay the rent: 425 fr. to the New Year, and
> politely give up the lodging. . . . In a few weeks you shall have a
> Ballade, a Polonaise and a Scherzo.

There are numerous letters with requests to deliver music, post letters, collect money, buy furniture, negotiate fees.

Chopin had known Fontana for such a long time that he allowed a less attractive side of himself to show. We like to think only of Chopin the tortured artist, but in his letters to Fontana we see the businessman, who did not want to see his art be undervalued. In one instance, when Chopin was unhappy with his business dealings with Camille Pleyel, he instructed Fontana to take his new pieces to Maurice Schlesinger instead. Privately, he referred to problematic business contacts as "Jews," as in: "Probst is a rascal to pay me 300 for the mazurkas! . . . I would rather sell my manuscripts for nothing as in the old days, than have to bow and scrape to such fools. And I'd rather be humiliated by one Jew than by three." Or "My Dear: If they're such Jews, hold back everything until I come." In choosing Schlesinger to publish something over Pleyel, Chopin said, "If I have got to deal with Jews, let it at least be Orthodox ones." In these letters, we glimpse many things including Chopin's desire to micromanage his friend's help, and also a mercurial temperament. After worrying that Pleyel was underpaying him, Chopin—in the very next letter—asks Fontana to make sure the Preludes were dedicated to Pleyel. He also requests that Fontana make sure that the Ballade be dedicated to Robert Schumann (which he misspells "Schuhmann" in the letter) and that Fontana himself be the dedicatee of op. 40.

When Chopin and Sand prepared to return to Paris, Chopin asked Fontana to find apartments—with very specific requirements, to decorate, and buy and install furniture. He was expected to order Chopin's clothes and pick them up, and again be responsible for all of the details of Chopin's hats, pants, and coats. Chopin showed a little bit of haughtiness in the way he referred to Fontana—who never refused a request from Chopin—to others. He would call him dismissively his *totumfacki*, a twist on the Latin *factotum*, which means "one who does all." His relationship with Fontana shows a less than endearing portrait of Chopin. His careless anti-Semitism is particularly tasteless, and is miles away from the excessively polite persona he cultivated for his friends in the elite class. Still, Chopin was an imperfect human, and consequently we must accept the flaws as they are without making excuses for them.

In defense of Fontana, who showed vast reserves of patience dealing with the most flawed version of Chopin, we should remember him not as Chopin's *totumfacki*, but as a successful musician in his own right. He was the director of the Havana Philharmonic Society in Cuba, and he was the first person to bring Chopin's music to the island. After Chopin's death, the composer's mother and sisters gave Fontana permission to edit the works Chopin left behind. They became opp. 66–73 (completed in 1855) and op. 74 (from 1859). Fontana's final years were quite tragic, indeed, and we might wish that they were more comfortable. He was widowed in 1855 and subsequently lost his hearing. Unable to continue with music, he became more involved in literary pursuits, translating *Don Quixote* into Polish. Near the end of his life he struggled with deafness and also poverty when he could not take control of his wife's estate after her death. He committed suicide in 1869, leaving his son in the care of his wife's family in England.

AUGUSTE FRANCHOMME

Chopin reserved a special place in his heart for his Polish compatriots. He was more wary of others, although it was by and large his new friendships that made him a success in Paris. When Chopin arrived in Paris, he carried two letters of reference: one from Jósef Elsner to Jean François Lesueur, and one from Dr. Johann Malfatti to Ferdinando Paër. Through these letters, Chopin met Gioacchino Rossini, Giacomo Meyerbeer, Friedrich Kalkbrenner, Franz Liszt, Henri Herz, Ferdinand Hiller, violinist Pierre Baillot, and cellist Auguste Franchomme. Liszt introduced Chopin and Franchomme, and the two immediately found that they had similar temperaments. It also didn't hurt that Chopin—whose affinity for the piano was to the exclusion of nearly everything else—was quite fond of the cello. Of the new friends he made shortly after arriving in Paris, Franchomme has the distinction of becoming one of the closest. In fact, author Pierre Azoury calls him "the most intimate non-Polish friend" of Chopin.

Parisian society was quite taken with Giacomo Meyerbeer's opera *Robert le diable* when it premiered in that city at the end of 1831. Chopin too, who had barely been in Paris for two months at the time, was impressed by the work. Publisher Maurice Schlesinger approached Chopin and asked him if he might be tempted to compose some variations based on music from *Robert le diable*. The result was the 1832–1823 collaboration between Chopin and Auguste Franchomme. The virtuosic Grand Duo Concertant sur des Thèmes de Robert le diable for Piano and Cello was published in 1833 (without an opus number). It explores three main themes from Meyerbeer's opera. It is intensely dramatic in parts and shifts moods and colors often. As something of a duet of ideas, the work doesn't fit perfectly with Chopin's emerging style, and indeed, the composer omitted it from his own list of compositions, although the *brillante* piano solo at the beginning could hardly have been composed by anyone but Chopin. And Chopin arranged the Grand Duo Concertant for four-hand piano in the 1830s.

In 1833, Chopin endeavored to become a successful composer in Paris. He took on more students, and formed a salon with his new non-Polish friends. They'd meet for dinner and then head to either Chopin's apartment or Liszt's place to play music late into the night. He also tried to publish as much as possible. He spent summer holidays with Franchomme near Tours, and he referred to his friend by the familiar pronoun, which was a rare thing among his non-Polish friends. In 1844, when Chopin lost his father, George Sand implored Franchomme to be the one to comfort him.

Chopin's Sonata for Cello and Piano in G minor, op. 65 was composed for, and dedicated to, Franchomme. Chopin wrote it in 1846, and it was the last piece of Chopin's that was published while he was alive. The sonata is constructed in four movements, with an opening Allegro moderato, followed by a Scherzo in the second movement, a lyrical Largo as the third movement, and a dance-like rondo finale. The music in this work is very dramatic, with sudden shifts of mood, and in the hands of two excellent players, it can feel like a catharsis. Although adhering to the basic shape of sonata form with its two contrasting themes and developmental center section, Chopin takes some liberties, and the result is an emotional presentation. The initial theme has the flavor of a march, and the second subject provides a brief shift into lyricism. Although there is beautiful simplicity here, Chopin often has three melodies going at once, with one in each hand of the piano and one for the cello. In fact, we may characterize this first movement by its passionate dialogue between the piano and cello. The second movement is a quick scherzo in a minor key, and Chopin eschews gloom and doom here for a spirited display by both players. The trio section moves away from the quickly traded short passages of the scherzo and instead offers longer phrases that seem to dance. This central section also provides contrast with a lengthy excursion in the major mode.

The subsequent Largo movement isn't even thirty measures long, but what it lacks in length it makes up for with deeply felt emotion. It is by turns both yearning and hopeful. The lively Allegro finale demonstrates Chopin's refined sense of rhythm. The piano and cello seem to spur each other on, and this skillful interplay between the instruments makes one wonder what might have been if Chopin had continued to compose for another ten or twenty years. Performances of the Sonata op. 65 usually take around thirty minutes, and there are few pieces in Chopin's output of this depth and size.

In addition to being one of Europe's most enchanting cellists, Franchomme was a composer. He wrote a concerto for cello, Caprices, études, and pieces for cello and orchestra. He also transcribed some of Chopin's work to be played by cello and piano, like the op. 55 Nocturnes and the B-flat minor Sonata. He was evidently a very attentive friend as well. He handled details with Chopin's publishers from 1844 to 1846. At Chopin's last public recital in Paris, in February of 1848 (at the salon of Pleyel), Franchomme performed as part of a piano trio by Mozart, and he played the last three movements of the Cello Sonata with Chopin. Franchomme was there for Chopin's final illness, and was a pallbearer at the funeral. After Chopin's death, Franchomme continued their connection. His own daughter Cécile was a piano student of one of Chopin's students (Camille Dubois, née O'Meara). Franchomme played for Chopin's students, and helped publish some of the composer's posthumous works.

FRANZ LISZT

Upon Chopin's arrival in Paris, it became clear to the composer that a public concert would help grow his reputation. A solo recital was not something that appealed to the Parisian audience, so a variety of acts would have to be assembled and presented in a suitable venue. It was not Chopin's strength to pull together all of the things such a concert would need, but he pressed on, nevertheless. Among his first new contacts in Paris were fellow composers Hector Berlioz and Franz Liszt. On the outside, Liszt and Chopin must have seemed like polar opposites, with Liszt the extrovert enjoying the spotlight and Chopin the introvert avoiding the stage. But they shared a Romantic sensibility, and they enjoyed playing together at the piano.

Liszt and Chopin had a period of relative closeness, but on the whole enjoyed a friendship of circumstance. They had friends in common, visited the same salons, even played together in public more than half a dozen times. Liszt was a flamboyant performer and very public figure, generally. This was at odds with Chopin, who strove to cultivate an aura of class and a quiet, dignified public persona. At times, Chopin admired Liszt's musicianship; at other times Liszt's playing was too much for Chopin, who put a high value on sensitivity and expression. Author Xavier Jon Puslowski claimed: "Chopin's perfect control was anything but the outsized symphonic sweep Liszt was practicing a la Paganini. But even if Chopin's tolerance for Liszt's over-exuberant congratulation was limited, at the time, he did appreciate its sincerity. For the next few years, a 'companionship of opposites was struck.'" Chopin dedicated the op. 10 Études to Liszt.

Liszt is a fascinating creature in his own right: dazzling performer, innovative composer, dynamic conductor, trusted teacher, and champion of his fellow musicians. Liszt's fame put him in a unique position to endorse and support up-and-coming composers, and he used this power often. His relationship with Chopin was certainly beneficial for Chopin, and opened more than a few doors. They were born just a year apart (Liszt in 1811), and both started giving concerts as children. But while Chopin's public appearances as a child were something of a novelty, Liszt's performance career was serious from the first. At one performance, Beethoven supposedly kissed the young man on the forehead. Liszt also tried his hand at composition; at the age of eleven, he was the youngest composer asked to contribute to the anthology of Variations on a Theme by Diabelli (the same theme for which Beethoven composed thirty-three dizzying Variations). In fact, this was his first published work. When his father died in 1827, Liszt gave up touring to teach. Things might have ended there; Liszt might have ended up being a piano and composition teacher for the rest of his life, but his unique talent emerged at a fortuitous time. Liszt and his mother were living in Paris in the 1830s, an artistic crossroads, and it was here in 1832 that Liszt had occasion to see a performance by noted Italian violin virtuoso, Niccolò Paganini. It was after this event that Liszt decided to become a virtuoso on piano. Paris was the perfect place for this as some of the most forward-thinking pedagogues and performers lived and worked in the city. Liszt showed uncommon talent for the new techniques, and soon he was rising head and shoulders above his contemporaries.

To show off his growing talents, Liszt began to transcribe orchestral works for piano and perform them. With these, he accomplished two things: he furthered his own reputation as a performer, and he championed the work of other composers. He transcribed some of Beethoven's symphonies, although Beethoven's reputation needed no help from Liszt, but he also undertook a transcription of Hector Berlioz's five-movement epic, *Symphonie Fantastique*. Liszt's efforts benefitted Berlioz as much as they did Liszt himself. The score to *Symphonie Fantastique* had not been published at the time, and Berlioz was not yet recognized in France for his genius. *Symphonie Fantastique* went on to become a great favorite in the repertoire, as it remains today. If you've ever heard this incredible piece, you might wonder how Liszt was able to distill the essence of Berlioz's massive orchestral piece into a two-hand piano piece. It can't have been easy, but the work is a feat of both masterful transcription and virtuosic performance.

In 1839, Liszt began what would be an eight-year tour of Europe. In this time, the fan response to his playing—and even his presence in a particular city—began to border on frenzy. The term "Lisztomania" is credited to poet Heinrich Heine, who wrote about the phenomenon in Paris in April of 1844. The first recorded incident of "Liszt fever" took place near the end of 1841, in Berlin. Before he'd even played a note, a group of students serenaded the composer with his song "Rheinweinlied," and later reacted with considerable commotion when Liszt gave a recital on December 27. In this day and age, such overly ardent passion for celebrity is commonplace. But in the 1840s, this kind of behavior was unusual, to say the least. Among some of the alleged actions of a Liszt-addled crowd: rushing the performer before and after performances, vying for the odd discarded handkerchief or glove, attempting to obtain locks of his hair, wearing his portrait on jewelry, and making bracelets out of the piano strings he often broke in performance.

Because the suffix "-mania" has been used so often since—"Beatlemania" is a perfect example—we take it to mean, in this context, evidence of somewhat extreme, but ultimately harmless, celebrity worship. But in the nineteenth century, the term "mania" was a specific medical diagnosis. This distinction has been strongly made by musicologist Dana Gooley in the book *The Virtuoso Liszt*. Instead of being a quaint pastime of enthusiastic youth, Lisztomania was a described as a pathological condition, one that was contagious. Gooley describes the purely physical reaction due to the overstimulation of Liszt's playing (this effect was seen primarily in the youthful German audience):

> [Liszt's] high-intensity, often frantic bravura manner provoked involuntary physical reactions—shaking, shuddering, weeping. Applause for Liszt, indeed, appears less a gesture of appreciation, wonder, or joy, than a sheer corporal reflex—an outlet for great physical excitement.

Liszt himself was likely surprised by the ardent reactions of his audience. Perhaps he was even frightened by them. On the one hand, Liszt's extraordinary playing and his personal charisma must have given the youth of Berlin and other cities an outlet for their energy and passion. On the other hand, Liszt's charitable work (he was a great philanthropist and humanitarian) and his personal warmth were held up as a way to defend such vehement fervor for the artist.

One of Liszt's important romantic relationships was with Marie d'Agoult, a countess who was six years older than Liszt. The Countess d'Agoult was the dedicatee of Chopin's op. 25 Études. Marie d'Agoult, who was born Marie Catherine Sophie de Flavigny, married Count Charles Louis Constant d'Agoult in 1827. They had two daughters but divorced in 1835, when she left the count to be with Liszt in Geneva. She and Liszt lived together from 1835 to 1839, in Switzerland and Italy primarily, and in that time, the two did not marry, but had three children. Their daughter Cosima was married twice, first to pianist and conductor Hans von Bülow, then to opera composer Richard Wagner. Marie d'Agoult was a writer, and published most of her works in the 1840s. Like her contemporary George Sand, she wrote under a pseudonym, Daniel Stern. It was under this name that she published her most successful work, the three-volume *Histoire de la revolution de 1848*.

Liszt's touring schedule made him internationally famous, fabulously wealthy, and a legend, but strained the relationship between Liszt and Countess d'Agoult. In the eight years that Liszt tirelessly toured Europe, seeing his children (and their mother) mostly in the summers, he played multiple concerts weekly. The grand total of concerts Liszt performed during these years is likely a thousand. Compare this with the thirty that Chopin performed.

Liszt was also something of a cad where matters of the heart were concerned. While involved with Countess d'Agoult, Liszt also had a short affair with Camille Pleyel's wife, Marie. She was very beautiful and talented and quickly became part of the Parisian musical scene in the 1830s. Chopin dedicated his op. 9 Nocturnes to her. Marie Pleyel (née Moke)—who had herself perpetrated infidelities that ended her marriage to Pleyel after four years—had previously been the central infatuation of Hector Berlioz. In fact, when Berlioz found out that Marie was going to marry Camille Pleyel, he hatched a plan to kill the lovers. The plan was thwarted by some lost luggage which allowed Berlioz time to come to his senses. Liszt's affair with Marie Pleyel caused a rift with Chopin. Around 1833, Liszt and Marie Pleyel had a secret encounter at Chopin's apartment at the Rue de la Chaussée d'Antin. This incident—ostensibly not sanctioned by Chopin—caused a rift in their relationship. Perhaps Chopin felt unjustly used or perhaps he was troubled by Liszt's treatment of Countess d'Agoult. Perhaps he was hurt on behalf of Camille Pleyel, with whom he enjoyed a warm friendship, for the most part. Liszt's relationship with Countess d'Agoult survived this infidelity, but finally came to an end in 1844.

Liszt's next important relationship would start in 1847, when he met Polish royalty, Princess Carolyne zu Sayn-Wittgenstein. Sayn-Wittgenstein would be a very influential figure in Liszt's life, and helped him to focus his energy on creating rather than touring. At the age of thirty-five, his concert career was over, and this was quite sad for the public, but it meant that Liszt could channel his energies into creativity. It also meant that he left the stage a legend. He settled in Weimar to conduct,

teach, and write. He continued to champion the works of other composers, like Wagner (who would become his son-in-law). He and Sayn-
Wittgenstein attempted to marry—near his fiftieth birthday—but her
first husband, with the help of the Tsar of Russia, made that impossible.
They remained involved with each other for decades, and she ghost-
wrote several of Liszt's publications, likely including the biography, *Life
of Chopin*. This particular volume was published in the 1860s and
thereafter translated from the original French into English by Martha
Walker. Constructed as it is in overly ornate prose, *Life of Chopin* is
more a meandering rumination on Chopin—perhaps gleaned from con-
versations between Liszt and Sayn-Wittgenstein—than a strictly factual
account.

In his later years, Liszt returned to thoughts of a religious life—an
idea that his parents discouraged when Liszt was young—and joined
the Third Order of St. Francis. He lived in Rome, simply and alone,
leaving his extravagant youth behind him. At this point, Lisztomania
must have seemed like a distantly remembered fever dream. He continued to travel and teach, with some interruptions for illness, until his
death at the age of seventy-four.

When Chopin was living with Jan Matuszyński, the two would often
entertain. Liszt was one of their regular visitors. The two men would
debate over ways to play piano pieces of the day, including their own
works. Indeed, Chopin admired the way that Liszt played his études,
noting in a letter to Ferdinand Hiller, "I would like to steal from him his
way of performing my own creations." The men played three concerts
together in 1833. The first was put together by Hector Berlioz as a
benefit to help his fiancée, Harriet Smithson. For that concert, the men
played the Sonata in F minor op. 22, four hands by George Onslow. In
the second concert, Liszt and Chopin joined Henri Herz and others in
various virtuosic works for one- and two-piano. In their third concert
appearance for the year, they played Bach's Concerto in D minor for
Three Harpsichords (BWV 1063). They obviously played pianos instead
of harpsichords.

In the 1834–1835 season, Chopin played two concerts with Liszt. On
Christmas of 1834, the two appeared at an event at the Salle Pleyel that
had been organized by music critic François Stoepel. Liszt and Chopin
played Ignaz Moscheles's Grande Sonate for four hands in E-flat, op.
47, and Liszt's two-piano arrangement of Felix Mendelssohn's *Lieder*

ohne Worte. A few months later, in April, the two performed at a benefit concert sponsored by the Benevolent Association of Polish Ladies in Paris. On this program, the duo played a two-piano piece by Hiller.

Liszt transcribed a number of Chopin's pieces. He transcribed Chopin's Mazurka in C-sharp minor, op. 6, no. 2 for violin and piano, sometime in the years 1832–1835. Over a decade after Chopin's death, Liszt transcribed Chopin's Préludes for organ. Records show that Liszt did an organ, cello, and piano transcription of the third movement (Marche Funebre) of Chopin's Sonata No. 2 in B-flat minor, but this piece has unfortunately been lost. Documents also show that Liszt planned to transcribe the Fantasie in F minor as a piano and orchestra piece, but this transcription never came to fruition. Liszt did take six of Chopin's songs and make a set of piano miniatures with them, *6 Chants polonais*. He made a few minor musical modifications to make them flow together better.

Although Chopin made a name for himself, there's no doubt that his association with Franz Liszt certainly helped smooth his way into Parisian society. In the 1945 film *A Song to Remember*, Liszt's small but important role in Chopin's life is dramatized in two scenes. Upon Chopin's arrival in Paris, it is Liszt's performance of Chopin's music, a polonaise—which he happens upon by chance in Pleyel's showroom—that convinces Pleyel to give the young and unknown Chopin a public concert at his salon. Unfortunately, the concert goes poorly because of Chopin's emotional reaction to some bad news from Warsaw, and it seems his career in Paris is over before it had even begun. George Sand and Liszt have a plan, however, and invite Chopin to a party at the house of the Duchess of Orleans. At this soirée, the crowd is delighted when it is announced that Liszt will play a piano solo. Liszt requests that the room be darkened for his performance, and he begins to play, or so the audience thinks. Even the servants and footmen outside stop to listen to the legendary Liszt playing a new piece. "Anything will sound good played by Liszt," remarks Kalkbrenner. The transfixed audience is then given quite the surprise when George Sand slowly walks up to the piano from the back of the room with a candelabra. The light illuminates Chopin playing the piano and not Liszt at all. The audience applauds rapturously, suddenly understanding that there is another legend in the room. Liszt then appears to proclaim Chopin "one of the greatest artists of all time." His fame and reputation are assured, thanks to the help of his friends.

4

CREATIVE NOCTURNES

In this chapter we look at Chopin as a creative and expressive force. We discuss the idea of rubato, a musical technique common in Romantic piano music that relies on expressive use of rhythm. We attempt to get to the heart of his compositional process, focusing specifically on the nocturnes, a genre he wrote between 1827 and 1846. And no discussion of nocturnes would be complete without mention of the Irish composer, John Field, pioneer of the genre, and a man whose pianistic style influenced young Chopin.

CHOPIN'S COMPOSITIONAL PROCESS

For nearly ten years, George Sand and Chopin were companions, creating their respective arts side by side, as it were. Sand was one of the few people who saw Chopin in the throes of creating new musical works, and—like nearly everything else she experienced—described his struggles in florid verbiage. She painted a picture of a compositional process both arduous and painstaking. The completion of a work might take place days, weeks, months, or years from its initial inspiration. Sand describes the onset of inspiration and the commencement of a new work "spontaneous and miraculous." This initial burst of creativity was followed by a "heart-rending labor." One publisher, Maurice Schlesinger, remarked, "Chopin still worked on creations finished a long time ago."

In fact, this constant struggle was challenging for publishers who often waited for new works for months or even years. Chopin labored to meet deadlines set by pre-sale agreements or commissions, but sometimes failed to do so. At times, the perfectionist in him would hold back a work indefinitely if he deemed it unsuitable for public consumption. In fact, before his death, Chopin asked that all of his unpublished work be burned, but this was a directive ignored by his loved ones. Indeed, many works were published after Chopin's death in 1849, including one published as late as 1968. Chopin's compositional process is at the heart of his nocturnes, which were written between 1827 and 1846. Although these works were not published in strict chronological order, they still outline an overarching pattern of development that reveals an artist constantly in search of innovation and unique expression. Like all patterns of maturation and refinement, this development is not rigidly linear, and Chopin's movement toward an artistic ideal in the nocturnes has unexpected twists and turns.

THE LONELY CHRISTMAS

Chopin arrived in Vienna on November 23, 1830. He was traveling with his childhood friend, Tytus Wojciechowski. They first stayed at the City of London Hotel (Zur Stadt London) in the Fleischmarkt area of the city. A few days later they moved to the Golden Lamb Hotel (Zur Goldenen Lamm) by the Prater, a large public park northeast of the city center. Finding both of these options too expensive, they eventually found a furnished three-room apartment on an upper floor of a building that was even closer to the center of Vienna and more affordable. This was the beginning of what would be Chopin's eight-month stay in Vienna. Tytus's early departure left him alone, but Chopin consoled himself by going out most nights, meeting new people and experiencing the musical culture of Vienna. In addition to seeing operas and other performances, he had occasion to meet Anton Diabelli, of the eponymous Variations; he made the acquaintance of Josef Merk, first cellist of the Viennese opera, to whom Chopin would dedicate his Introduction and Polonaise Brillante for piano and cello, op. 3; he also met the doctor and music lover, Johann Malfatti. He reconnected with Carl Czerny and Johann Hummel while in Vienna as well.

Chopin worked on a number of pieces in this time. He had already written two nocturnes back in Warsaw, and he continued to develop this genre in Vienna and later in Paris as well. While we're not certain what occupied his writing time in December of 1830, we know that a melancholy mood pervaded his letters from that time. This was a time of transition and turmoil for the twenty-year-old composer and we might be inspired to let our imagination paint a picture of a single day.

We know of some of the events mentioned below because Chopin wrote a letter to his dear friend Jan Matuszyński on December 26, 1830. In this letter, he describes spending time with a fellow Pole in Vienna saying, "I love to go there for the reminiscence; all the music, the pocket handkerchiefs and table-napkins all have her name on them." Of his gloomy walk to St. Stephen's he tells Jaś, "I never felt my loneliness so clearly." After returning to his apartment after his lonely walk, he reports dreaming of friends and family. He was conflicted about what to do next, seemingly stuck in the middle, so to speak, between his old life in Warsaw and his new life in Paris.

It is December of 1830. Christmas approaches and Chopin sits alone in his room in Vienna. Being alone is difficult, especially since Tytus left to return to Warsaw. The circumstances of his departure were stressful, as political turmoil in Warsaw enticed both Fryderyk and Tytus to return home to fight. Tytus had convinced Fryderyk to stay in Vienna, but it was a difficult parting, neither knowing if they would see the other again. So Chopin sits at the piano, trying to compose. In his melancholy mood, perhaps he is sketching. Let's imagine that he is sketching out the beginning of a piece in B-flat minor. The opening line in the right hand is plaintive and expressive, while the left-hand accompaniment provides a gentle, but steady feeling of rocking. The piece is taking the shape of a nocturne. Even the meter he has chosen lends itself to the nocturne idea. It's in 6/4, a compound meter that relies on a feeling of seesawing between two sets of three beats in each measure. Meters of this type have historically been used for lullabies and songs about boats. Chopin's melody line starts very simply and returns with ornamented complexity, a recurrent thought that spins out, like a worry. The center section in a major key might display a more hopeful mood, if the composer can conjure up such a feeling in these circumstances.

Chopin anxiously waits for news from family and friends in Warsaw; not knowing if they are safe is heartrending. As he pens another mournful phrase—this one expressively fits twenty-two notes where twelve should fit—he contemplates his first Christmas away from family, away from his parents and sisters. He prays for their safety and hopes he will see them again soon. He is thankful at least for the friendly Polish people in Vienna like Konstancja Bayerowa, who has Fryderyk over frequently. He has Christmas dinner planned with the Malfatti family. Dr. Malfatti is married to a Polish woman who is quite fond of Fryderyk, so he will at least be around the Polish language he loves and the traditions he already misses. He takes a gloomy walk down to St. Stephen's cathedral and feels quite alone, but reminds himself that it will soon be 1831. Chopin has great hopes for the new year and for his future. He turns against the wind and heads home, to write some more.

TEMPO RUBATO

An important musical aspect of many of Chopin's pieces is a rhythmic practice used in some of the solo piano literature of the Romantic period called rubato. *Tempo rubato* literally means "stolen time" in Italian. It is a designation that first appeared in the 1720s indicating that a player should alter the rhythm in a measure (or across measures) as an embellishment. The time would soon rebound back to "normal," resulting in not so much stolen time, but borrowed time. In practical terms, such rubato is only possible in solos or very small groups. Solo pianists and guitarists, for example, are most likely to use rubato in their performances, since there are no other musicians with whom to keep time.

In his book *Stolen Time: The History of Tempo Rubato* (1996), Richard Hudson outlines two types of rubato: first, the late-Baroque type, which was confined to the melody, while the accompaniment kept strict time (Hudson calls this "earlier rubato"), and second, the rubato that developed in the Classical and Romantic periods, which could be felt in all aspects of a musical piece; that is to say, both melody and accompaniment were affected by the flexible approach to rhythm. Hudson called this type "later rubato." Works by Chopin are often today performed in this second kind of rubato, where all aspects of the music are equally altered; however, that was not what Chopin himself advised. Rather, he seemed to want the left hand to keep strict time while the right hand took some rhythmic liberties, the earlier type of rubato. A student of Chopin, Wilhelm von Lenz, remembered his teacher's words: "'The left hand,' I often heard him say, 'is the Kapellmeister: it mustn't relent or bend. It's a clock. Do with the right hand what you want and can.'" Some have suggested the influence of Italian opera on this practice, as singers in operas by Rossini, Bellini, and so on would normally have demonstrated a degree of rhythmic liberty against an orchestral part that was mostly unyielding. Certainly, Chopin's extensive experience of operas from Vienna and his first years in Paris would support such a theory; however, we don't know that for sure as he simply did not speak about it specifically.

JOHN FIELD

One of Chopin's influences as pianist and composer was Irish composer and pianist John Field (1782–1837). Born into a musical family, Field's father was a violinist and his grandfather was an organist; the latter was also his first teacher. In Dublin, Italian composer Tommaso Giordani— whose family formed a small, traveling opera troupe—took on young John Field as a student for what turned out to be a year. That year, the year Field turned nine, he performed three public concerts in Dublin, garnering positive reviews from local press. The Field family decided to move to London in 1793. It isn't known whether Giordani helped make arrangements with Field's next teacher, Muzio Clementi, but the two did know each other and occasionally worked together. Regardless, when the Fields arrived in London, young John soon had a new teacher. Robert Field, John's father, worked as a violinist at the Little Haymarket Theatre in London. By late summer of 1793, John Field was giving his first public performance in the city featuring the performance of a concerto (we don't know which one). In addition to taking piano lessons, Field also took lessons on the violin. By the time he was eighteen years old, his virtuosity on the piano was known all over London, and he played concerts often.

Clementi, whose music is discussed in chapter 1, was thought of as the "father of the piano," not only because of the idiomatic compositions he wrote for the instruments, but also because he was a maker of pianos. Clementi used Field's skills to help sell his product. By 1802, the two men traveled together to various cities, including Paris and

Vienna, where there were opportunities for selling Clementi's pianos, making connections with potential patrons, and finding additional educational support for Field (like counterpoint lessons in Vienna). Field found great opportunities for teaching and performing in St. Petersburg and remained there after Clementi's departure. He stayed in Russia and eventually made an impressive debut in Moscow in 1806. Field had meanwhile been building up a portfolio of pieces for publication including piano concertos, sonatas, and variations. Most of these pieces were first published in London and Paris, and later in Russia. It was in Moscow that Field developed what has been called his "post-London style." Part of this development included the influence of some music that Field encountered from about 1807–1811: Dussek's piano sonatas (particularly opp. 61, 70, and 75) and folksong collector and composer Daniil Kashin's publication of the *Zhurnal otechestvennoy muzïki* (*Journal of National Music*), which included Russian folk tunes.

Field's first compositions after hearing these other pieces reflect their influence. In 1808–1809, Field composed variations on Russian folk tunes. He had also developed a different texture described as "chromatically decorated coloratura melody accompanied by sonorously laid out left hand and pedal." It is this texture that crystallized in the first of the seventeen nocturnes that Field would compose. Field returned to St. Petersburg with visits to Moscow and spent the next few years writing many of his most important works. His Russian publisher, H. J. Dalmas, put out these works as well as revised editions of the works that had been published previously. Field also shortly thereafter began a successful collaboration with Breitkopf & Härtel, who published Field's work in Europe.

Although his reputation as a dazzling performer traveled far and wide, by 1823, he was scaling back on his public appearances as a pianist. He continued composing and even reworked a couple of his nocturnes for voice and piano. By the 1830s, his health became a deciding factor in his next move. Field was reportedly a man of voracious appetite for both food and alcohol, and his "outrageous" behavior began to take its toll on his body. Suffering with rectal cancer, he undertook a concert tour that would take him to Manchester and London, where he would receive an operation. There he had the opportunity to meet Felix Mendelssohn and Ignaz Moscheles. Field's visit also coincided with the death of Clementi in March of 1832; Field was a pallbearer at the funeral. Later that year, Field premiered Concerto No. 7 in Paris on December 25, 1832. The reviews for this piece were mixed, owing more to the evolving tastes of the music-going public than to a decrease in Field's abilities. He met Liszt and Chopin while in Paris, the latter having arrived in Paris in 1831.

Field could have been a bombastic presence at the piano, showing off bravura passages of fast-moving notes and intricate counterpoint. Instead, he chose a much quieter persona at the keyboard. This choice of emphasis on musicality, phrasing, and tone is in evidence in his own pieces, many of which opt for a generally quiet and introspective mood. Contemporary accounts, including those of his students, praised his distinct but soft touch. Mikhail Glinka, one of the nineteenth century's foremost Russian composers, took three lessons with Field shortly after arriving in St. Petersburg at the age of thirteen. He described Field's playing thusly: "It seemed that he did not strike the keys but his fingers fell on them as large raindrops and scattered like pearls on velvet."

Franz Liszt also had an opinion of Field's playing, which he wrote out at length. In speaking specifically about the nocturnes, Liszt remarks on how fresh they seem, even decades after their composition. He also speaks to the delicacy of Field's performance at the keyboard, noting that Field's contemplative style reveled in subtlety. Without explicitly saying it, Liszt seemed to be drawing a comparison between his own crowd-pleasing style and Field's seeming "indifference." Liszt said, "It is not hard to see that he was his own chief audience. His calm was all but sleepy, and could be neither disturbed nor affected by thoughts of the impression his playing made on his hearers. . . . Field sang for himself alone." It was because of this, Liszt argued, that Field was among the first to place emotion before structure:

> Before him [piano pieces] all had of necessity to be cast as sonatas or rondos or some such. Field, contrariwise, introduced a genre that belonged to none of these existing categories, in which feeling and melody reigned supreme, and which moved freely, without the fetters and constraints of any preconceived form.

As such, Field was the progenitor of a style that allowed for pieces like Mendelssohn's *Lieder ohne Worte* and of course many of the genres favored by Chopin, including the twenty-one nocturnes Chopin contributed to the world.

Because Chopin is the better known of the two, where Field is mentioned, Chopin is usually nearby. In fact, there are some sources that connect the two men as the alpha and omega of a particular piano style. The 1980 version of *The New Grove* states: "[Field] was the originator of an important school of Romantic pianism that culminated in Chopin." The later edition from 2000 backs off this connection a bit, saying: "He was the originator of the Nocturne and of the style of pianism regarded as 'Chopinesque.'" Certainly the playing styles of both men had something in common, namely a sensitive touch that relied on dexterity, innovative fingerings, and emotional acuity. Another important similarity between Field and Chopin was the singular voice they found with the piano; with very few exceptions, the output of each man contains no significant contributions to the literature of other instruments. Field wrote more piano concertos (seven) than Chopin (two), but this is certainly because Field played more public concerts, which virtually required this genre as a showpiece for piano soloists. Finally, the two are connected by the nocturne, which was Field's gift to solo piano literature.

Field had considered other names for his new genre that emphasized atmosphere over form and mood over function. We might now be having a slightly different discussion if he'd chosen "Pastorale" or "Serenade," but these would have brought with them their own associations. The term "nocturne"—an evocation of the night—is vaguer and therefore more open to interpretation. Field's first nocturne appeared in 1812, and he continued to compose them through the 1830s. Since the nocturne is not constrained by the limitations of an established form, what we notice as a unifying factor is the stratification of the roles of left and right hand. In these works, the left hand acts as steady accompaniment, while the right plays a melody, sometimes heavily ornamented. In terms of mood, the nocturne has been described as embodying the spirit of "sadness consoled." Chopin adhered to this division of the labor between left and right hand, although he took them further afield (and indeed, further *than* Field) with hymnlike sections, quasi-recitatives, and more dramatic gestures.

Because of Chopin, Field's nocturnes have received the most notice of all of his works. They have overshadowed the rest of his work in the eyes of history. This incomplete picture of Field is somewhat unfair, as his work in other genres is valid and influential. His Russian-inspired piano works from the early nineteenth century, for example, certainly shone a light on the path Russian nationalists would take in later generations, led by Glinka and followed by Mily Balakirev and Nikolai Rimsky-Korsakov.

THE NOCTURNES

Chopin's choice to call some of his works "Nocturnes" begged comparison with the work of Field. When Chopin's first set of nocturnes were published, critic Ludwig Rellstab weighed op. 9 against Field's nocturnes and found in favor of the Irish composer:

> Where Field smiles, Chopin makes a grinning grimace; where Field sighs, Chopin groans; where Field puts some seasoning into the food, Chopin empties a handful of pepper. . . . If one holds Field's charming nocturnes before a distorting, concave mirror, one gets Chopin's work.

Pianist Moscheles complained that the restlessness of Chopin's nocturnes caused him to lose sleep. Chopin wasn't interested in mimicking Field's style, but rather using the older nocturnes as a point of departure. Although he admired Field's work and his playing, Chopin was never interested in sounding like anyone but Chopin.

Chopin composed all of his nocturnes between 1827 and 1846. Most of them were published when Chopin was alive, but two were published posthumously. The numbering of the nocturnes is therefore not strictly chronological. Like Field's nocturnes, Chopin's nocturnes maintain the primary melody in the right hand and the accompanying chords in the left hand, but there are slight deviations from this from time to time. Chopin also uses rubato rhythm and more pedal to add dramatic weight. Although each of Chopin's nocturnes is unique, he generally used an ABA form in which the repetition of the "A" was highly embellished and the "B" section outlined a contrasting mood. There are exceptions, of course. A couple of the nocturnes have no B section to speak of, and sometimes both the A and B repeat. The moods of the nocturnes may be characterized by melancholy or pensiveness, and Chopin chose the tempos of *Larghetto*, *Lento*, and *Andante* (one of them is marked *Allegretto*). We also see some influence of vocal music in the use of the occasional marking *recitativo*.

We begin at the end; the op. 72 Nocturne was published posthumously, but it was written in 1827, before Chopin had even left Warsaw. It was his first foray into the genre and represents a lovely exploration of a simple sorrowful theme that gives way to a hopeful center section. While this composition would have been a charming achievement for another composer, Chopin felt that it was not good enough to be published so it remained hidden from the public until after his death.

Chopin began the op. 9 nocturnes during the eight-month period he spent in Vienna, but completed them after moving to Paris in 1831. The Nocturne in B-flat minor, op. 9 no. 1 is a wonderful example of the established nocturne style. The extremely expressive right hand part feels almost improvisational, as simple melodies return in ornamented form. One might assume from the rubato and the style that the player is simple *feeling* these embellishments, but Chopin painstakingly notated every one of these seemingly extemporaneous lines. The left hand part remains steady with a regular rhythm that never relents (until the third from last bar), although the quiet mood of the piece never allows that steady pulse to feel imposing.

The second Nocturne in the set, op. 9, no. 2, like the first one, was dedicated to Camille Pleyel. This one has some similarities (same key, similar left hand part, cadenza-like passage in the final section) with Field's Nocturne No. 9. This is one of the best-known nocturnes by Chopin. The third one in the set is performed and heard less often, but it is the most complex one of the group. There is a great deal of pent-up energy in the right hand part, which bursts forth—relatively speaking—in the *agitato* middle section. The final cascade down from the very high register in the last few bars washes away any sense of agitation, and the piece ends softly and peacefully.

Chopin dedicated the op. 15 Nocturnes to German conductor and composer Ferdinand Hiller. Chopin seems to be playing with the idea of contrast in the middle sections of these works, and the greatest sense of conflict and peace occurs in the Nocturne F major op. 15, no. 1. One reading could be that the quietest of nights is interrupted by a thunderstorm. The return to the *sotto voce* theme of the opening is all the more effective for having followed the sudden "cloudburst." The second in this set of three, the Nocturne in F-sharp major, op. 15, no. 2, cultivates a serene mood throughout, even in the center section, which encourages a slightly more urgent sense of movement, but still never approaches agitation or even storminess. The third and final Nocturne in this set plays by its own rules. There is an anecdote that Chopin was inspired to write this piece after seeing a production of *Hamlet*, and even considered naming it "At the cemetery" or "In the Graveyard." This is uncharacteristic of the composer, who hardly ever overtly discussed his inspirations, but it's a good story (and we recount it here) so it persists. It certainly feels different than the other Nocturnes both in this set and those in op. 9. The form is somewhat dissimilar as well, with a hymnlike center section marked *religioso*, which gives way to a third part that does not return us to the opening theme. Rather, there is a new melodic idea, and indeed a new key. Chopin slides back into the original tonality of G minor for the final few bars, closing the circle, albeit in a slightly unexpected way.

The two Nocturnes of op. 27 were composed in 1836 and 1837 and dedicated to Countess d'Appony. One gets the feeling that with these works, Chopin had developed past the original idea of the nocturne put forth by Field and was slowly and steadily moving into a realm all his own. Chopin's biographer Niecks was rather fond of these Nocturnes, considering them the cream of the crop. Whether it is their sense of drama or pensive personal emotion that sets them apart, they are certainly innovative. The pair of Nocturnes in op. 32, composed in the same years as op. 27, lack some of the gravitas of the earlier opus number, but still provide some interesting features. The ending of op. 32, no. 1 is actually quite surprising; Chopin marks a "coda" and then proceeds to have the piano declaim something in a passage marked *recitativo*. It is a delightful and unexpected touch. Op. 32, no. 2 is notable because it actually had a second life as part of a ballet. In 1909, Alexander Glazunov orchestrated a number of Chopin pieces (some originally in a suite from 1892 called *Chopiniana*) for a non-narrative ballet called *Les Sylphides*, choreographed by Mikhail Fokine. Other pieces in this work include the Waltz in G-flat major and the Mazurka in C major.

Chopin composed the subsequent pair of Nocturnes of op. 37 in the late 1830s and the pair in op. 48 in the early 1840s. With these four

Nocturnes, Chopin continued to experiment with the form, even reaching beyond what one might consider the outer boundaries. Op. 48, no. 1 especially has been noticed for its stunning emotional gravity. More than one scholar has described this as more of a ballade than a nocturne. Some of the words used when describing this piece include "grief," "nobility," and "imposing." Chopin scholar Jim Samson also notes "a dramatic decline in [Chopin's] rate of production" that coincides with the writing of op. 48.

The two nocturnes of op. 55—dedicated to pupil Jane Stirling—again push the boundaries of the nocturne form and even against the structures Chopin had laid out in previous explorations of the form. Op. 55, no. 2 in particular has no contrasting middle section, instead relying on a continually evolving melody. The two nocturnes of op. 62 date from 1846. Op. 62, no.1 revels in declamation, perhaps even in the idea of storytelling. Op. 62, no. 2 shows off true dramatic range, with agitation and tension eventually calming and settling. These two works chart a slight departure from what one might come to expect from a nocturne. Although their quirky charms have made them interesting for study and an important signpost for how far Chopin had taken the genre, the pair turned out to be something of a disappointment for Niecks and others, as if Chopin had gone past his prime. They were the last nocturnes Chopin published and among the last pieces he completed before his death.

Nocturne No. 20 in C-sharp minor was published posthumously. It has no opus number, but it was composed in 1830, forty years before its publication in 1870. It has some thematic ideas in common with the concerto Chopin was writing at the time. Marked *Lento con gran espressione* (and sometimes referred to as such), Chopin dedicated it to his sister Ludwika as "an exercise before beginning the study of [Chopin's] second Concerto." Some have nicknamed the work "Reminiscence" because of its sense of yearning and nostalgia. This is a hauntingly beautiful work, and one of the most used nocturnes in popular culture. It appears in the film the *Peacemaker*, in the television show *The Killing*, and in the video game *Dying Light*. It was also played on screen (twice) in the 2002 Roman Polanski film *The Pianist*. Adrien Brody received an Academy Award for his portrayal of protagonist, Władysław Szpilman (1911–2000). The film opens with Szpilman playing Chopin's Nocturne No. 20 in C-sharp minor live on Warsaw radio, a performance interrupted by Nazi bombing. This is a true aspect of the story; Szpilman was indeed playing Chopin's Nocturne in C-sharp minor on September 23, 1939. His performance was interrupted by German artillery, and it was the final live performance on Warsaw radio for the next six years. One might imagine so poignant a gesture to be an invention of the screenwriters—Polish voices (represented by Chopin and Szpilman) silenced by the Nazis—but it is true. The music of Chopin stands in for the musical voice of a country that lost so much, and Szpilman's miraculous survival keeps that voice alive until the end of the war. Near the end of the film, Szpilman has been restored to his position as house pianist for Warsaw Polish radio, which has been restored. Just as he had in real life, the Szpilman of the film plays the C-sharp minor Nocturne, completing the circle. What makes this nocturne such a perfect choice (besides being the actual piece that Szpilman played) is that its passionate and mournful theme transitions into one that is more hopeful for the center section, and even when the sad A theme returns, it is considerably lightened by a major chord at the end. It somehow mirrors the quality of our experience: sadness gives way to contentment, and sunshine touches melancholy. Such was Chopin's own life, and he wrote it well.

5

DEVOTION TO POLAND

Chopin was very proud of his native Poland, and in his final days it must have weighed heavily on his mind that he was never able to return there after his departure as a twenty-year-old. He lived half of his life in Paris, and he adapted well to life there, but he never fully left Poland behind. Besides maintaining friendships with many fellow Poles who lived in Paris, Chopin wove Polish folk music into his compositions, forever linking him to the culture of his native country. Who Chopin was as a person and an artist was no doubt influenced by the political climate of Warsaw in the 1820s, and this chapter is an exploration of some of the ways in which Chopin developed an understanding of Polish culture from both a musical and political standpoint. For the sake of context, we begin with a brief history of Poland under the tsar. The central focus of this chapter, however, is Polish dance forms, and how they influenced Chopin's compositional style. Chopin's friend Pauline Viardot was in turn influenced by some of the composer's mazurkas, creating vocal versions of fifteen of them. We round out this chapter with a discussion of these works.

POLAND UNDER THE TSAR

By the early nineteenth century Poland found its land divided into partitions for Russia, Prussia, and Austria. The Duchy of Warsaw was created by Napoleon in 1807, and ruled by the King of Saxony, as outlined in the treaty of Tilsit. This Duchy, allied with France, was challenged in 1809 when war with Austria began. Allied troops fought back against the invading forces, and the resultant Treaty of Schönbrunn expanded the land of the Duchy further south. In 1812, Napoleon began a campaign against Russia. Ultimately unsuccessful, the Duchy fell to the Russians in early 1813. The Congress of Vienna in 1815 redrew the map of Europe, giving the Duchy of Warsaw (except for the Poznań region, which went to Prussia, and Kraków) to Tsar Alexander. This region became known as the Kingdom of Poland. In November of 1815, the kingdom was granted a constitution, which allowed it to elect its own parliament. Although Tsar Alexander I never officially became the king of Poland after the Congress of Vienna, he installed his younger brother Constantine (whose title was Grand Duke) as the viceroy of Poland. The autonomy enjoyed by the kingdom was worn away gradually, and by 1819, most of the freedoms it had initially enjoyed were gone, including freedom of the press. Alexander also had his secret police root out opposing groups. The Freemasons, for example, had shown opposition to the monarchy, and had their activities suspended via an edict issued in 1821. The constitution was formally replaced with the Organic Statute in the wake of the Polish uprising of 1830–1831, and this document did away with both the parliament and the army.

The fate of Poland in the early part of the nineteenth century was uncertain, and this was not helped by the instability in Russia, especially after the sudden death of Tsar Alexander in 1825. In normal circumstances, Alexander would have passed on the mantle of power to his own son, and failing that, his younger brother Constantine. But when he succumbed to typhus at the age of 47, it was not immediately apparent who would take over as he had no heir and Constantine was not much interested in the role. Constantine served in the military, but did not involve himself in politics. After one failed marriage, he wed a Polish woman, Joanna Grudzińska, in 1820, and subsequently unofficially renounced his claim to the throne. Tsar Alexander had another brother, Nicholas, who was born in 1796, the youngest of the three.

When Alexander died on December 1, 1825, it was uncertain for twenty-five days which of the brothers would become emperor. When Constantine formally refused, Nicholas ascended to the throne, retroactive to the date of Alexander's death. The day after his accession, the Decembrist Uprising took place in Imperial Russia.

The Decembrists, as they were called, grew out of a political party called the Union of Salvation, which later became the Union of Prosperity (UoP). The UoP favored a move from autocracy to a constitutional form of government. Some factions of the UoP sought to bring about this change by peaceful means, while others favored a forceful turnover of power. The more radical wing of the party also supported the redistribution of land and the abolition of class divisions. One of the individuals in this radical faction was Pavel Pestel. He was a rousing speaker who had inspired many men to the cause. Surmising that peaceful protests would not emancipate the serfs—one of the central causes of the UoP—Pestel saw an opportunity in the commotion after Alexander's death.

On December 26, 1825, a force of 3,000 dissenting soldiers stood in Peter's Square (now Senate Square) in St. Petersburg, where Nicholas lived in the Winter Palace. These troops refused to proclaim allegiance to Nicholas, and waited to be joined by their leader, Prince Trubetskoy, Colonel Bulatov, and other soldiers who felt the same. The Decembrists waited in vain. The opposing group of loyalists boasted many more soldiers than the rebel force. The two sides squared off for hours, without much happening. Nicholas I emerged to quash the rebellion using artillery. In Tulchin, in the south, Pestel was arrested for treason. He and four other revolutionaries were hanged for this crime. A monument to these men sits on the execution site in St. Petersburg.

Back in Poland, political opposition to Russian rule fomented over the next few years, culminating in an uprising in November of 1830. In this November Uprising, as it came to be called, the cadets of Poland's military academy—led by Piotr Wysocki—revolted against the Russian forces. They attacked Belweder Palace, the seat of the Grand Duke Constantine, but the Duke escaped before any harm could come to him. The uprising was not alone in its efforts; factions from Lithuania, Belarus, and Ukraine joined the Polish cadets. By the next day, the Polish forces had pushed the Russian troops to the north of Warsaw. The Russian army ultimately ended the conflict with its far greater numbers, although the conflict—known as the Russo–Polish War after the parliament passed the Act of Dethronization of Nicholas I—went on for nearly a year. In response, Nicholas declared Poland a part of Russia, minimizing its internal systems and closing Warsaw University.

Alexander I and his brother Nicholas I held additional titles as King of Poland and Grand Duke of Finland. Nicholas was a conservative ruler, who quashed political dissent in all forms. During his reign, Russia expanded into more territories, including modern-day Armenia and Azerbaijan, which were wrested from Persian forces in the Russo-Persian War. He secured victories for Russia in numerous conflicts, but in doing so depleted its coffers. He died in the midst of the Crimean War, a face-off that would prove disastrous for Russia.

CHOPIN THE NATIONALIST

As a young man, Chopin's considerable talent garnered the notice of many rich and powerful people. In 1825, a newspaper in Warsaw reported that Chopin played for Tsar Alexander, who happened to be visiting the city. Chopin reportedly did so well in the performance, the tsar gave him a diamond ring. He had previously played for the tsar's mother in 1818, when she visited the University and the Gymnasium. On this occasion, Chopin played two Polish dances.

In the 1820s, Chopin was a frequent guest at Belweder, the palace where Grand Duke Constantine stayed while in the city. Constantine's son Paweł lived at Belweder, and he sometimes brought Chopin to the residence for social calls. The Grand Duke apparently enjoyed Chopin's company as well, and it was said that the young composer's gentle performances helped ease his agitated temper. Although Chopin knew many people who would participate in the November Uprising, he still brought a letter of support from the Grand Duke when he visited Vienna. Chopin's ideas about politics were very quietly forming throughout the decade 1820–1830. He seemed to understand the delicate balance at play, and his visits with members of the Russian royal family certainly influenced how outspoken Chopin might be on political matters, which is to say that Chopin was officially mum on the subject, at least in mixed company.

Other experiences influenced him as well. During the summers of 1824 and 1825, Chopin was invited to Szafarnia to stay with a school friend, Dominik-Jan-Henryk Dziewanowski, known as "Domus" to his friends, on vacation. Chopin seemed to have a wonderful time, writing cheerful letters back home to his family. He called his letters "The Szafarina Courier" and wrote them in the style of the Warsaw newspaper. These visits turned out to be formative experiences for Chopin, who heard the folk music of the countryside and participated in country celebrations. This music would become important in Chopin's style, especially in the polonaises and mazurkas.

In addition to small performances in Warsaw, Chopin went to Berlin with family friend Feliks Jarocki in 1828, and the following year he went back as the guest of Prince Antoni Radziwiłł. The prince was a musician, a cellist, and his daughter Wanda was a pianist. To them Chopin presented a piece for cello and piano, Introduction and Polonaise Brillante in C major, his op. 3. Going on these small trips and getting some press allowed Chopin some more opportunity to travel to new places. When Chopin returned from his first concerts abroad in Vienna in 1829, he wandered about Warsaw contemplating his next move. What he heard around him was a general unrest about Tsar Nicholas I, whose rule in Poland was proving to be more and more oppressive.

By late 1830, Chopin left Warsaw for Austria, but within weeks of his departure, the November Uprising erupted. Chopin, who was traveling with his boyhood friend Tytus, stayed in Vienna, while his friend headed back to enlist. Chopin expressed regret about not returning to enlist, but Tytus smartly convinced him to stay put. Chopin's role in the revolution would not be as a physical presence in battle, but instead a symbolic standard-bearer of the Polish culture as he traveled through many of the important cities in Europe. Privately, he confessed worry and feelings of impotent anger at the events. In the aftermath of the November Uprising, when Polish forces had been defeated, Chopin wondered about his family's safety and privately lamented, "Why could I not have slain even a single Muscovite!"

Chopin's correspondence of the time, especially to his family, never refers directly to the political events happening in Poland. Some have interpreted this as a disinterest in the political affairs of his native country, but that was not the case, of course. He was smart to be careful, as letters were read and censored. His position outside of Poland, although certainly safer in some ways, was precarious. He was at the mercy of the bureaucracy for his passport, for example. When he finally made it to Paris in 1831, he found the lifestyle quite suitable, especially when he began teaching and making important friends. In 1833, the tsar offered amnesty so Chopin could conceivably have returned, but his career in Paris was just getting off the ground, and a return to Poland would have seemed like a step backward. He chose to stay, and he would never set foot on Polish soil again. He was not alone; there was a thriving community of Polish expatriates in Paris, and Chopin became a favored member of that group. Chopin played benefit concerts for Polish refugees. The combination of experience of Polish folk culture and the political tumult in his homeland became an important part of his identity as an artist. Polish historian and composer Zdzisław Jachimecki described this process as causing Chopin's development into "an inspired national bard."

Composer and music journalist Robert Schumann grasped the implications of Chopin's music, saying that Chopin was a dangerous enemy of Tsar Nicholas. In a review Schumann wrote in 1836 of Chopin's Piano Concertos, Schumann writes—under the guise of his pseudonym, Eusebius—that Chopin's work "follows the voice of Beethoven" because of its genius. He mentions the current political climate: "Now that the Poles are deep in mourning, their appeal to us artists is even stronger." He goes on to say that Paris was the right choice for Chopin as it allowed him free rein to both compose and rage. "For if the mighty autocratic monarch in the north could know that in Chopin's works, in the simple strains of his mazurkas, there lurks a dangerous enemy, he would place a ban on music. Chopin's works are cannons buried under flowers!" He also goes on to say that for Chopin to be truly great, he would have to let some (although not all) of that nationalistic spirit go: "the more he distances himself from it, the more significant will he be for the art as a whole." In his article on Chopin in the collection *Nineteenth Century Piano Music*, Jeffrey Kallberg argues that Chopin's connection with his native country—the concept of which has been kept alive by Chopin biographers and other commentators—tells us that in hearing the music of Chopin, we are in some sense, "hear[ing] Poland."

NATIONAL DANCES

The name "mazurka" links the dance with the province of Mazowsze, a low-lying section of central Poland dotted with forests. The dances from this area, known generally as mazurkas, are actually a few slightly different types of dances: the *mazur* or *mazurek*, the *obertas* or *oberek*, and a dance from the Kujawy region, called the *kujawiak*. Both the *mazurek* and *kujawiak* are named for neighboring regions, while the name of the *oberek* derives for the verb meaning "to spin." All of these national folk dances have a triple meter and strong accents. Dancers performing these dances might mark accents by tapping their heels to the floor or stomping on the downbeat. Of the three types, the *oberek* usually has the fastest tempo, and requires dancers to spin and jump, sometimes in couples, sometimes in a circle. There are also parts of the dance for the women only and certain steps—usually the most athletic leaps—for the men. In some performances the *oberek* is prefaced by a *kujawiak*, which is a slower, more stately dance. Although *obereks* seem the most joyful and playful, the mazurka in general was able to convey many disparate moods from elation to melancholy. Certainly Chopin captured many moods in his exploration of the genre. Chopin's Mazurka in E minor, op. 17 no. 2 draws upon the *kujawiak*, for example, while the *oberek* inspired the Mazurka in D major of op. 33 (no. 2).

Like most dances, there are repeated sections in the basic structure, sometimes two to four. The resulting patterns of traditional dances might be laid out as AABB form or AAAB. The sections themselves are in turn made up of six or eight measures. When Chopin composed mazurkas, he was less concerned with maintaining the strict structure of sections that would accommodate actual dancing. Some mazurkas extend the length of sections, as his own artistic vision warranted. Also important to Chopin's work in this genre was rhythmic flexibility, specifically the use of rubato (discussed in chapter 4), which allowed for temporal elasticity based on the interpretation of the soloist. In other words, the performer does not have to stay strictly in time (a directive called *rubato*). It is also important to note that Chopin stopped short of using any actual mazurka tunes. Other composers writing in a nationalistic spirit set preexistent folk tunes in their work. Béla Bartók was one such composer who, in the twentieth century, created settings for dozens of Hungarian folk tunes. But Chopin preferred to create new tunes from whole cloth, rather than reworking established folk tunes.

The mazurka spread to other parts of Poland and into neighboring countries in the seventeenth century. It appeared in Germany, then France, and then England. From there it crossed the Atlantic and reached the United States. When Poland was partitioned by Russia, the mazurka traveled to Russia through the courts and out among the people. Before Chopin, fellow Polish pianist Maria Szymanowska composed mazurkas in the 1820s. Some Russian composers also took up the genre. In the late nineteenth century, Alexander Borodin included the mazurka in two movements of his piano collection *Petite Suite*. The form was also explored by Mikhail Glinka, Alexander Scriabin, and Pyotr Ilyich Tchaikovsky. In the 1920s, Karol Szymanowski proved himself the heir of the authentically Polish mazurka, publishing over twenty pieces that drew upon the mazurka and its variations. For musical compositions inspired by the mazurka that do not have the structure of the dance, composers would write *"alla mazurka"* as a designation.

The mazurka in the nineteenth century was elevated into the realm of art music in part because of Chopin. He composed possibly seventy mazurkas for piano, although there is disagreement about the actual number. Only fifty-eight have been published: forty-five during his lifetime and thirteen posthumously. Many of these were published in eleven collections: opp. 6, 7, 17, 24, 30, 33, 41, 50, 56, 59, 63, 67 (posth.), 68 (posth.); two others were published on their own. The others that are thought to exist are assumed to be in private collections.

Chopin began writing mazurkas in the 1820s, when he was a teenager. It's one of the few genres that Chopin wrote throughout his life. There was an intensification of his efforts in this genre after the political events of 1830. In July of 1831, Chopin wrote a letter to his family while he was waiting in Vienna to make the move to Paris, speaking of the Viennese. "I don't even know how to dance a waltz properly. . . . My piano has heard only mazury." In a review of the mazurkas in 1838, Schumann said the oft-quoted line: "Each of the mazurkas has an individual poetic feature, something distinctive in form or expression." Hector Berlioz observed that the Polish elements added "something natively untamed . . . that charms and captivates by its very strangeness." In his mazurkas, Chopin mimicked the distinctive rhythms and repetitive structures while also maintaining musical elements we've come to associate with Chopin, like interesting harmonies and contrapuntal textures.

While Chopin was developing as an artist and composer, nationalism was growing as an important musical force in the nineteenth century, with other artists striving to reflect national character in their work.

There was also a surge of exoticism, with audiences becoming fascinated with musical styles from foreign lands. We can see this attitude in the F minor Piano Concerto, which Chopin composed for his initial travels outside of Poland. The mazurka-inspired final movement was likely composed with two things in mind: Chopin's own cultural identity and the "exotic" musical fare favored by the Parisian and Viennese audiences. Not everyone was a fan, however. Critic Ludwig Rellstab reviewed Chopin's first two collections of mazurkas, noting "ear-splitting dissonances, tortured transitions, piercing modulations, disgusting dislocations of the melody and rhythm." One of the compositional choices Chopin sometimes made was to write in modes that included slight variations to the major and minor keys that make up the bulk of Western music. Chopin's use of the Lydian mode—with its raised fourth—was disorienting for some listeners.

In addition to mazurkas, Chopin also wrote polonaises, which were solo piano pieces inspired by a Polish dance in triple time. The term "polonaise" can either refer to the Polish dance, or to a piece inspired by the style, mostly developing outside of Poland. The defining feature of a polonaise is a particular rhythm. It is a triple-meter dance (like the mazurka), and in this type, the traditional rhythm is as follows: beat one has one long and two short rhythms (an eighth and two sixteenths), beat two is split into two even eighth notes, and beat three is also two eighth notes. Obviously, music based primarily on such a rhythm could vary widely. As Polish nationalism began to grow in the wake of political turmoil at the end of the eighteenth century, the polonaise took on "a heightened emotional quality with contrasts between noble majesty and heartfelt melancholy," although polonaises could also be virtuosic and brilliant. The dance itself was normally performed at carnival parties and at student dances. It still has a place in modern Poland, where the processional dance is still part of proms, graduations, weddings, and other celebrations.

Chopin composed his first polonaise when he was just a child of seven, and his last dates from just a few years before his death in 1849. Of the twenty-one or so (accounts differ) polonaises we believe Chopin wrote in his lifetime, there are a few thought lost. Seven were published when Chopin was alive, and nine were published posthumously. One of the most famous polonaises is the Polonaise-Fantasie of 1846. It is a complex work of virtuosity that Chopin conceived as a fantasy first. The aspects that suggested polonaise must have emerged as Chopin was composing. Chopin was not the only composer who used the designation *alla polacca*. Other works with this include pieces by J. S. Bach, C. P. E. Bach, Mozart, and Schubert.

PAULINE VIARDOT AND THE MAZURKAS

One of Chopin's close friends was Pauline Viardot, a pianist, composer, and successful mezzo-soprano. She was born into a musical family; her father was the famous tenor Miguel García, who also taught and composed. Her sister—more than a dozen years older—was celebrated mezzo-soprano Maria Malibrán. Viardot was a gifted pianist, and wanted to make a career as a concert performer. One of her piano teachers was Franz Liszt; with Anton Reicha, who taught Liszt and Berlioz, she learned composition. After the death of her father, her mother insisted Viardot concentrate on the voice and leave piano behind. After the untimely death of her older sister, Viardot became a professional singer at the age of fifteen, making her opera debut at seventeen as Desdemona in Gioachino Rossini's *Otello*. She became friends with George Sand (and was supposedly the inspiration for Sand's serial novel of 1842–1843, *Consuelo*) and other writers of the time. Her marriage to Louis Viardot, who was twenty-one years her senior, produced three children. Louis Viardot also managed his wife's professional career. In 1843, Russian writer Ivan Turgenev, then twenty-five, fell in love with twenty-two-year-old Pauline. He spent the rest of his life living near the Viardot family or in their house with them. There are questions about the nature of the relationship, but some modern scholars believe that Pauline Viardot and Ivan Turgenev might have shared a long-term affair with the knowledge and approval of Louis Viardot. Regardless of their personal connection, they also enjoyed a fruitful artistic collaboration.

Pauline Viardot was one of the inner circle of Chopin and George Sand, visiting them at Nohant, playing piano and trading knowledge with Chopin. Viardot produced vocal arrangements of fifteen of Chopin's mazurkas; six were published in 1848. They are fascinating pieces with beautiful and complex vocal lines, although Polish musicologists uniformly say that Chopin did not approve of these versions. There are many sources, however, that mention Chopin freely giving Viardot advice on the best way to arrange these pieces. Chopin mentions the mazurka arrangements in a few letters from 1848, and in each case, seems either neutral or positive about them. In one to Wojciech Grzymała from July of 1848, he says, "Yesterday (July 7th) I gave a second matinée in Lord Falmuth's [sic] house. Mme Viardot sang me my mazurkas among other things. It was very beautiful." Now, we cannot know what was said in confidence or felt in the heart, but at least on paper, Chopin gave no overt disapproval. If he *had* disliked the arrangements, the poetry was probably partly to blame. Musicologist Mieczysław Tomaszewski called the texts by Louis Pomey "superficial and arch-banal."

The songs themselves are quite lovely, and the intricacies of the vocal line certainly mimic the turns and embellishments of Chopin's piano part. While at first listen the songs might seem charmingly simple, there are some interesting demands made on the singer, like agile changes in direction, rising glissandos, and long-held trills. When Viardot died in 1910, her music faded from view and was mostly forgotten. Recent efforts have attempted to provide exposure for the talents of this extraordinary woman, whom Liszt praised as both a pianist and a composer. In 2006, Opera Rara hosted an evening of her music featuring mezzo-soprano Frederica von Stade. The program, curated by television producer Judy Flannery (who considered making a documentary about Viardot) was presented at Britain's Wigmore Hall. And in 2013, author Barbara Kendall-Davies published a new biography of Viardot, *The Life and Work of Pauline Viardot Garcia.*

6

LOVE, CHOPIN STYLE

Chopin was not born to love one woman.

—George Sand

A SNAPSHOT OF THE HALCYON DAYS IN NOHANT

We begin this chapter with a picture. It is a sneak peek into Chopin's longest relationship with a woman. This woman, George Sand, would be central to Chopin's life for almost a decade. It must have seemed like an odd arrangement to some, the celebrated female writer who went by a male name and wore men's clothes with the perfectly coifed dandy, Chopin. Although they spent years in each other's company, oftentimes living together (and certainly, they were romantically involved for some of those years), they never discussed marriage or any formal declaration of their connectedness. But at its apex, their relationship worked beautifully.

Sand's summer home in Nohant is about 180 miles south of Paris. It is now run by the *Centre des monuments nationaux* and is open to the public. One can visit the estate and see where Sand penned many of her novels, where Chopin composed, and where Sand herself played as a child. The gardens are especially beautiful, and the house is filled with Sand's furniture and belongings, donated by her descendants. Oh, to stand in those rooms and imagine the creative energy that must have permeated every inch of that space!

Sand spent a good deal of time in Nohant, and Chopin spent seven summers there with her. As two creative artists, summer vacation was time to write and compose, and although sometimes they entertained guests and relaxed, these two souls were most content when working at their respective arts. Perhaps their compatibility in that realm is what kept them together for so long. On a typical summer day in Nohant, their schedule was as follows: Sand would sleep in in the morning. She would socialize in the afternoon, and write from the evening into the wee hours of the night. If she was on a roll, she would work until dawn, finishing up her writing and walking down to the river to lie naked in the water as the sun rose. Then she'd return to the house for sleep. At her most prolific, she averaged twenty longhand pages a day, the product of six or seven hours of concentrated writing. Not only did she produce novels by the dozen, but was a champion letter writer, with nearly 20,000 pieces of correspondence to her credit. Chopin, on the other hand, woke up early in the morning, composed throughout the day, received guests and socialized in the early evening and went to bed, just as Sand was beginning her "day" of writing. Sand described evenings in which Chopin would play to her "in the twilight," and then go to bed at the same time as her children.

This work schedule proved quite productive for Chopin who, during this time, completed the op. 41 Mazurkas (a set of four), the F-sharp major Impromptu, the G major Nocturne, and portions of the B-flat minor Sonata (the Funeral March part was already complete). Chopin's room was on the first floor of the house, and its windows faced south onto the lawn. Its walls were covered with red and blue wallpaper, and it was an airy, relaxed space. Sand observed his creative process from a distance, not wanting to disturb the delicate energy that allowed him to compose. She noted that the melodies came to the piano spontaneously. Her rapturous description of his "miraculous" composition described a process that she obviously felt privileged to witness. Perhaps she understood that to ask Chopin to have a conventional relationship with her would have upset his process, so she often stepped aside to let him go through it. And it was sometimes "the most desperate labour" as Chopin attempted to recreate on the page what had come to him so purely:

He analysed too much in trying to write it down, and his dismay at his inability to rediscover in it what he thought was its original purity threw him into a kind of despair. He would lock himself up in his room for whole days, weeping, pacing back and forth, breaking his pens, repeating or changing one bar a hundred times, writing and erasing it as many times, and beginning again the next day with an infinite and desperate perseverance. He sometimes spent six weeks on one page, only in the end to write it exactly as he had sketched at the first draft.

Despite Chopin's sometimes difficult process, these days of mutual creation were likely the best they enjoyed, with a rhythm they fell into easily. The flow was disrupted at times by Chopin's illness, and in their later years by some personal conflict, but the halcyon days at Nohant are worth remembering as an ideal of two artists living symbiotically, if only for a little while.

Chopin was admired by many women who enjoyed his gentility, his immaculate physical presentation, and of course his incredible talent. To the eyes of many, he cut an angelic figure—almost androgynous—from the smooth skin of his face to his slender build to his soft voice. Not too many women became romantically involved with Chopin, however, and those who did form a very small, exclusive group. We meet the ladies of this group, beginning with Chopin's boyhood crushes (with special mention of a male friend from his youth) followed by the woman who some thought Chopin would marry. While these other people certainly deserve to be mentioned, we spend most of this chapter getting to know George Sand, the person with whom Chopin would spend almost a decade. During their time together, Chopin had periods of great productivity, and one genre he undertook while with George Sand was the ballade, which we explore at the end of this chapter.

THE ANDROGYNOUS ANGEL

In Thomas Mann's *Doctor Faustus*, the protagonist Adrian Leverkühn ruminates on Chopin. "I love the angelic in his figure," he says, "the peculiarly and very mysteriously veiled, unapproachable, withdrawing, unadventurous flavor of his being." This is an assessment of his figure that resonates with the ones spoken and written by George Sand. In the

first stages of their "courtship," Sand wrote to their mutual friend Wojciech Grzymała about "this angel," Chopin. She would continually refer
to him in this way throughout their relationship. As his sickness wors-
ened, she sometimes called him a "poor angel." There is something
interesting in the way Sand viewed him. After he became ill on their
trip to Mallorca, she wrote to her friend, Charlotte Marliani, explaining
that she "care[d] for him like my child. He is an angel of sweetness and
kindness!"

It's very interesting to talk about the love life of a person who was
often described in terms of his androgyny because an angel, in this
context, may be viewed as a creature without sex: a pure being without
the crude flesh and desires of humanity. Jeffrey Kallberg, in his book
Chopin at the Boundaries, discusses this context and the image created
of Chopin—both in his own time and since—"as an androgynous, her-
maphroditic, effeminate, and/or pathological being." Likewise, Sand's
daughter Solange once referred to Chopin in a letter as *"sans-sexe,"* a
joking sobriquet that we might translate as "sexless." She called him this
when she was just thirteen years old, and there has been much speculation about the sexual feelings she may have developed for him just a few
years later.

In the 1990 film *Impromptu* (discussed in chapter 10), much is
made of this question of Chopin's identity. In their first face-to-face
meeting, George Sand says, "I'm delighted to find that you're not a man
at all, but an angel." Another character says, "I know the man. He's not
a man. He's a woman." Sand herself, when writing *Lucrezia Floriani*, a
novel with a male protagonist who shares some similarities to Chopin,
described the character of Prince Karol as follows:

> He remained physically delicate, as he was spiritually. But this very
> absence of muscular development had the advantage of preserving in
> him a charming beauty, an exceptional physiognomy which, so to
> speak, was without age or sex. . . . It was something like those ideal
> beings created by the poetic imagination of the Middle Ages to adorn
> Christian places of worship: an angel with the beautiful sad face of a
> woman, tall, perfect and slim of figure like a young Olympian god.

Of course, there has been much discussion over whether she had Chopin in mind when writing. Some say the resemblance is too similar to
have been accidental, and there is speculation that the publication of

this novel hastened the break between Chopin and Sand. Long after Chopin's death, Sand explained that Prince Karol was never meant to stand in for Chopin. "I have described, in my Prince Karol, the character of a man determined in his nature and exclusive in his feelings and demands. Such a man Chopin never was." Furthermore, she says that Karol was "a dreamer, nothing more; devoid of genius, he had not the rights of genius." Chopin was a great artist. "I never attempted to re-make any part of him. I respected his individuality as a I respected that of Delacroix and of my other friends who trod a different path than my own."

Clearly Chopin was a man of flesh and blood, with physical needs and desires, but held behind a veil. To some this boundary might simply have been his physical illness, to others his politeness and genteel nature. Chopin did hold people at something of an arm's length, making himself unavailable, but regardless of that, he did have his admirers. So the question remains, whom did this earthly angel choose to love? Upon which "mere mortals" did he bestow his affection? As we as humans no doubt understand, the ideal of love is usually so much more appealing than the love itself, which is often complicated, messy, and time-consuming. One biographer noted that Chopin seemed to thrive in the *idea* of a loving relationship, rather than an actual relationship. It helped him create: "There was obviously something in his nature which made him prefer fantasy to reality. He needed the exquisite ache of undeclared love to fire his inspiration."

BOYHOOD CRUSHES

The Chopin house was the family home, but was also a boarding house for some students of the Warsaw Lyceum, where Chopin's father Mikołaj taught. Tytus Wojciechowski was one of the boarders in the Chopin house in the fall of 1824. He was one of four boarders who would remain friends with Chopin for the rest of his life, although these two kept in touch mainly through correspondence. Tytus was two years older than Fryderyk, and was in many ways his opposite, the yang to Chopin's yin. While Chopin was thin and pale, Tytus was hearty and strong. Chopin was indecisive and uncertain, Tytus was calm and self-assured.

The bond between the fourteen-year-old Chopin and the sixteen-year-old Tytus was formed quickly. Chopin considered him a trusted confidant, and shared many thoughts and feelings with him. Chopin trusted Tytus enough to tell him that he had a crush on Konstancja Gładkowska (discussed below), a singer at the conservatory, but Chopin was also effusive in his feeling toward Tytus. It seems that theirs was a passionate connection. There's no proof of any physical interaction between them, but Chopin wrote to him things like, "I wanted to please you because I'm madly in love with you"; "Tonight you will dream that you are kissing me"; "I love you to distraction." Such uninhibited and unreserved writing was certainly common at the time, and Chopin was a particularly sensitive and demonstrative teenager. Chopin scholar Pierre Azoury, who wrote about Chopin's friends and contemporaries, said of this relationship: "There is no proof that Tytus and Chopin were ever lovers in the physical sense. It seems more likely that Chopin's *idée fixe* on Tytus was simply an extreme form of dependence." Chopin biographer Ruth Jordan states, "it would not be wrong to say that Tytus was Frederick's first love, in the confused and non-physical sense which is often characteristic of a first awakening."

After Tytus finished at the Warsaw Lyceum, he saw Chopin only a handful of times. Tytus studied law at Warsaw University from 1826 to 1829. In 1828, they saw each other at Konstanty Pruszak's country estate in Sanniki nad Wisła, and in 1830, Chopin visited Tytus in Poturzyn, where the Wojciechowski family had their land. Shortly after that the two traveled to Vienna. When the Polish uprising began in November of 1830, Tytus returned to Poland, while Chopin remained in Austria. Tytus was a second lieutenant in the Polish–Russian War, and was decorated with the Gold Cross of Military Virtue. In the 1860s, he was a leader in the White party. While Chopin turned to a career in music and his destiny in Paris and the world stage, Tytus continued his involvement in politics, and became a very successful agriculturist. He grew beets, adopted the practice of crop rotation, and eventually opened a successful sugar factory in Poland.

Tytus was the dedicatee of Chopin's Variations on Mozart's aria "La ci darem la mano," which was one of the very first pieces Chopin composed for the orchestra. After their parting in Vienna, Chopin never again saw his friend, but the two remained connected through letters. Decades after their meeting, in the final weeks of his life, Chopin thought of Tytus, who we might refer to in the words of today as Chopin's "man-crush." He hoped fervently to see Tytus again, but it was not to be.

In 1829, Chopin stood on the precipice of a new life outside of Poland. He was finishing up his education at the Warsaw Conservatory, taking his first tentative steps abroad, meeting important contemporaries (like Mendelssohn and Carl Friedrich Zelter), and composing some of his early masterpieces. It was also around this time that Chopin first noticed Konstancja Gładkowska, a mezzo soprano at the Warsaw Conservatory. He adored her from afar, calling her an "ideal." He spoke—in letters to others—about serving her "faithfully, though without saying a word to her, for six months." He actually met her a year after seeing her for the first time.

She was a talented singer, and her voice may have inspired his songwriting. Although he did not dedicate these works to her formally, Chopin composed eight of his nineteen known songs (five others have been lost) while she was in his life, so to speak. In early October of 1829, he composed the Waltz in D-flat major (op. 70, no. 3) with her in mind. He also imagined the slow movement of the Concerto in F minor was for her, although again, there was no formal dedication for her. In fact, when the Concerto was finally published, the dedicatee was Delfina Potocka. We know of these thoughts only because of a letter he wrote to Tytus on October 3, 1829. In this letter, Chopin mentions her not by name, but by referring to his "ideal," and goes on to explain that the thought of her inspired his creations: "in remembrance of whom was created the adagio [*larghetto* was the tempo he ultimately settled on] of my concerto, who inspired me to write that little waltz this morning, the one I sent to you."

Whatever their level of intimacy, it never rose to anything significant. She sang at his farewell concert at the Teatr Narodowy in October of 1830. He wrote rapturously to Tytus about her performance: "She sang the Cavatina from *La donna del lago* with recitative as she had never sung anything. . . . You know that *oh quante lagrime per te versai*. She uttered *tutto desto* to the lower B in such a way that Zieliński maintained that single B to be worth a thousand ducats." After his departure, they corresponded for a little while. He worried a bit for her after the suppression of the Warsaw Uprising. A little more than a year after Chopin left Warsaw, Konstancja married wealthy diplomat Józef

Grabowski. Chopin appears unaffected by the news and shared with Tytus that he never really felt more than "platonic affection" for her.

THE ENGAGEMENT

When Chopin arrived in Paris in 1831, his Polish passport did not allow him to travel at will. Upon receiving French citizenship in 1835, he was given a French passport, free to travel as he wished. He chose to surprise his parents, who were planning to spend a few weeks in Karlsbad. The three of them had a wonderful time together, and Chopin wrote to a friend that he was at the height of happiness. When they parted ways in mid-September, they could not have foreseen that it was the last time they would see each other. His parents headed back to Warsaw, and Chopin traveled through Dresden on his way to Leipzig.

While in Dresden, Chopin ran into childhood friend Feliks Wodziński. Feliks had been a student at the Warsaw Lyceum with Chopin, and the two families lived close together and enjoyed warm friendship. One of the daughters, Maria, was just a child when Fryderyk and Feliks were friends, but by 1835, she had grown into a beautiful young woman. Running into Feliks in Dresden, Chopin was informed that the family had moved. They invited him over. He stayed in Dresden longer than expected and spent a few days with the family. He entertained them by playing piano, of course. Maria and Fryderyk also spent some time alone, walking. She had been taking piano lessons in Geneva with pianist John Field.

Chopin wrote a short excerpt from one of his own Nocturnes (E-flat major, from op. 9) in Maria's album and dedicated a Waltz to her (A-flat major op. 69, no. 1). According to Jozefa Wodzińska (Maria's sister), Chopin played the waltz as he was about to depart for Leipzig. Soon after, Maria wrote him an emotional letter in French, which she had also been studying in Geneva. We do not know what Chopin said in response to this letter, but it appears that Maria was rather taken with the composer regardless. It seems Chopin had a very good time in Dresden, even though he wasn't in the best of health. When he finally finished his journey through Leipzig, as planned, where he met up with Mendelssohn, he arrived in Paris in mid-October. He crawled into bed with a respiratory infection that caused fever, excessive coughing, including the coughing up of blood. This was a frightening first for Chopin, but he recovered, and found himself in a decent state, mentally and physically, by 1836.

As a twenty-six-year-old man, an available bachelor, Chopin likely thought of marriage. Certainly by 1836 many of his friends were either married or about to get married. He seemed determined to return to Dresden in 1836, the invitation from the Wodzińskis open. But things were about to get more complicated. Rumors of Chopin's illness had traveled to Dresden, and when Maria's father visited the Chopins in Warsaw in December of 1835, he was a bit worried about Fryderyk's state of health. There was even a rumor of Chopin's death, which brought knowledge of Chopin's illness to the fore. Still, both families seemed happy that Maria and Fryderyk were becoming closer. In anticipation of spending time with Maria and her family, Chopin turned down invitations from Mendelssohn, Hiller, and Countess Marie d'Agoult. He spent most of August of 1836 with the Wodzińskis at Marienbad. His health was not perfect. He coughed quite a bit, and it was enough of an issue that Madame Wodzińska asked Chopin if he would consent to a medical examination by the Wodziński's family doctor.

After his departure, he received a letter from Maria's mother saying, "look after your health for everything depends on that." There is a question as to whether an actual proposal took place, but in any event, Madame Wodzińska decided that she would give Chopin a year to see if he—following doctor's advice—would improve in that time. Maria was ready to heed her parents' decision, whatever it would have been. Upon his departure from the family, Chopin gave Maria a "ring"—he wrote his song "The Ring," in her album, but they would not see each other again. Maria wrote to him a month later, "Adieu, until we meet again! Ah, let it be soon." The idea of marriage between Chopin and Maria seemed to simply dissipate. Chopin may have objected to Madame Wodzińska testing him for a year, or perhaps he was questioning whether or not he wanted a serious love commitment. In any case, the "engagement" with Maria left him a little wobbly, but was actually just one chapter coming to an end. In a sentimental mood sometime later, he labeled a stack of her letters *"moja bieda,"* "my sorrow."

GEORGE SAND

When we consider Chopin's relatively short life of thirty-nine years, we must realize that for much of his adult life, he merely flirted with the idea of a long-term relationship. To then understand that he spent almost a decade connected to a one woman—regardless of the unique circumstances of this relationship—reveals its singular importance. Chopin was involved with George Sand for fully one quarter of his life, one half of his adulthood. To get to the heart of this relationship, which was, for better or worse, the defining romantic relationship of Chopin's life, we must know the woman herself and her origins.

Before Aurore (the name George Sand was given at birth) was born, her parents had to meet, and she explains in her autobiography that her father, Maurice Dupin, was a military man from a good family, while her mother, Sophie-Victoire-Antoinette Delaborde, was "from an ugly and vagabond race of bohemians." She was thirty when she met Aurore's father. Maurice had been very close with his widowed mother, the two of them living at the family estate in Nohant, a small town south of Paris, in the center of the country. When Sophie met Maurice, they fell in love quickly, but Maurice's mother was not happy. In her autobiography, Sand describes her grandmother's tormented jealousy over her son's choice:

> It pained her to accept a daughter-in-law whose youth had been given over to frightening hazards. When she heard that her son had married my mother she was in despair, and wished to dissolve with her tears the contract cementing their union.

Maurice was caught in the middle of two women; to choose one would mean breaking the other's heart. It was only after the birth of young Aurore that there was an uneasy détente in the relationship between mother-in-law and daughter-in-law. When Aurore was barely a year old, Sophie left Paris to live near the camp where Maurice served. Aurore went to stay in the farming village of Chaillot, where Sophie's sister Lucie lived. Lucie's daughter Clotilde and Aurore were of similar age and temperament, and the two became close friends from their early childhoods. The two had vivid imaginations and they invented games that entertained them for hours at a time. Sophie further sparked her daughter's imagination with stories, myths, and fairytales. Soon Aurore was making up her own stories, cultivating an imagination that would spin entire novels from its golden silk.

Maurice returned to spend the winter of 1807–1808 with Sophie and Aurore. George Sand describes the family as loving and happy, but poor, although she did not feel deprived of anything. When Aurore was four, Sophie became pregnant with another child. Her husband was stationed in Spain, and Sand wondered if Sophie worried about his faithfulness. Sophie, with Aurore in tow, undertook a journey to meet up with him in Madrid, which was difficult as Sophie was seven or eight months pregnant. They stayed in Madrid about two months, during which time Sophie gave birth to a boy. The lightness of his eyes may have signaled blindness, but the real tragedy was still to come.

When Maurice was granted leave, the family of four set off for Nohant. Aurore suffered with a fever for part of the journey. They also traveled through countryside touched by battles, and shared their carriage with wounded soldiers. When they arrived in Nohant, Aurore's grandmother doted on her granddaughter, and she grew healthy again. But her brother's condition deteriorated. In a very telling passage in her autobiography, she said of this infant, "Watching him suffer, I began to love him. . . . I shared [my mother's] sorrow, and vaguely understood what worry is—that feeling so unnatural to children." Aurore's brother died, and the family was devastated. A little more than a week later, Maurice was killed while riding his horse home from a social engagement.

It was decided that Sophie would return to Paris to tend to her older daughter, Caroline (Aurore's half-sister), and leave Aurore at Nohant with her grandmother. This was a difficult decision, and Aurore felt torn between the love of these two women, much as her father had. Sand goes on to explain the troubled relationship between her and her mother. Although she had many fine qualities, Sophie could be short-tempered and hurtful. She was a "woman of contrasts," loved by many, but possessed of self-loathing. Sand sees the connection between them: "I am her imprint, but eroded by nature and altered by education."

Although she missed her mother, Aurore received an excellent education in Nohant, including the classics, and enjoyed the country life. She learned how to ride horses (she would wear boys' clothes when she rode), and helped with the upkeep of the property, tending to the chickens and lambs. Her grandmother also taught her to play the piano.

Aurore had a wild streak, and began to butt heads with her somewhat conservative grandmother as she got older. With no other alternatives, she resolved to send the young woman to an English convent that had been established on the Left Bank. Although Aurore held out hope to see her mother more often, Sophie was too engaged in her own life, and rejected many of Aurore's efforts to see her. Aurore did well at the school, which gave her a spiritual foundation, and she found a friend in her favorite teacher, Sister Mary Alice. At sixteen, she finished at the school and returned to Nohant, where she was able to forge a cordial rapport. She continued her education, learned more about managing the house and its affairs, and in 1821, when her grandmother died, she was ready to inherit the estate. She received an inheritance that made her independently wealthy, but what she truly wanted was a husband and family.

When she was eighteen, she married Casimir Dudevant, the illegitimate son of a baron who had known her father, Maurice. She soon became pregnant with their first child, whom she would name Maurice, and devoted herself fully to this marriage and her duties as wife and expectant mother. But her ideas about what marriage would be like were quite different from the realities of life with her husband. He was crude and loud, and she detested his physical attention. They hadn't much to say to each other; he did not share her love of literature or art, and spent most of his time drinking and hunting, leaving her alone most of the time.

She developed feelings for a lawyer named Aurélien de Sèze, whom she met on a family vacation. Unwilling to start a physical relationship with him, she instead gave Casimir an opportunity to become the man she really wanted. She outlined eight points that she hoped would make their marriage more harmonious. He agreed, attempting to read more, to give up his hobby of hunting, and to learn English. She maintained contact with Aurélien, which was part of the agreement with Casimir, although their relationship did not become physical. Soon, that connection petered out, and she decided—at the age of twenty-four—to have a proper extramarital affair.

Aurore had known Stéphane Ajasson de Grandsagne before her marriage. He had health issues, and Aurore obviously felt validated by taking care of him. Casimir knew of this affair, and she made no pretense of hiding it. When she became pregnant again, it was likely Stéphane's child. Solange was born in 1828. Casimir treated her like a daughter, although Stéphane also called her his daughter. Casimir was busy with his own affair with Pepita, the maid, even reportedly having sex with her while Aurore gave birth to Solange.

Aurore no longer slept in the same room as her husband, preferring instead to sleep in the room next to her children's rooms. She hired a male tutor with whom she may have been involved. She now likely had multiple lovers and a husband at home who had his own affairs. When Solange was a toddler, Aurore left her husband and marriage behind. For the next few years, she became romantically linked to Prosper Merimée, Alfred de Musset, Pierre-François Bocage, Felicien Malle-fille, and of course, Chopin.

The marriage with Casimir was over in every sense but the legal one, and Aurore longed to be in Paris, where art and politics lived. She told Casimir that she planned on spending half the year in Paris and half in Nohant. This agreement was based on the two of them maintaining their sham marriage. She drew a monthly allowance, hired a tutor for the children, whom she left in Nohant, and set on her way. The allowance wasn't much, but she began writing, hoping to make a living with it. She began dressing in men's clothing—for ease and comfort, but also because it was so much more economical, and also because it afforded her what she most craved, freedom.

She took another lover in 1830, a nineteen-year-old named Jules Sandeau. With Jules, it became apparent that Aurore had a "type." Slim, smart, younger men seemed to be her taste. These young men brought out the nurturing side of her. She called Jules "Le Petit Jules," and she once wrote about him, "if you knew how I love this poor child." Sand's first published stories were collaborations with Sandeau. Their chosen pseudonym was "Jules Sand." The two published *Rose et Blanche* in 1831. Her first solo novel was *Indiana*, published in 1832, using the name "George Sand" as her nom de plume. She produced constantly, bringing out new works, sometimes a few in a single year. For example, 1833 saw the publication of five novels: *Lélia, Andréa, Mattéa, Jacques,* and *Kouroglou/Épopée Persane*. In addition to publishing more than forty novels and a dozen plays, she was also the author of many nonfiction articles and memoirs. Some of her nonfiction writing included political work, especially in the realms of women's rights, and basic human rights for the poor and working class. She became particularly active during the 1848 Revolution.

She has been depicted in various forms as insensitive and brusque. She courted controversy when she began to wear men's clothing rather than the traditional dresses that were expected. She moved more freely through Paris because of this manner of dress. She smoked tobacco in public, which was also controversial at the time. However, it was within the social mores for a woman to live in a different place than the husband from whom she was separated. Her many affairs, though, made waves in certain social circles. Everyone seemed to have an opinion on how she was living her life, but she did as she pleased, unapologetically. She occupies a very unique and interesting space, characterized by a double gender identity. Other women used male pseudonyms for their writing, but it seems that only George Sand was thought of in both categories. One author described this phenomenon as the author "recognized as female but categorized as male, in the sense that Sand possessed the social resources and cultural power of a man. . . . 'George Sand' itself stood as a fictive category: it was a construct whose very name and whose very societal function worked to undo the fetters of traditional distinctions of gender."

When she met Chopin, she was immediately struck by him, but it took him a while to come around to the idea. She enlisted the help of a trusted friend. Sand and Chopin both knew Wojciech Grzymała, known as "Albert" to the Parisians. Grzymała was a Polish expatriate who had been a prisoner of war of the Russians. He had spent time in prison for being part of a secret patriotic society and for being part of the Decembrist plot. When his rebellious days were behind him, he became a wealthy banker and decided to live abroad in Paris, where he founded the Polish Literary Society, of which Chopin was a member. Grzymała, who was a music critic for *Kurier Polski*, was friends with George Sand. They met through the poet, Mickiewicz. Sand and Grzymała were actually very close friends, a fact they likely downplayed for Chopin's sake. In a letter Sand wrote to Grzymała she said, "I did not mention the fact to [Chopin] that I met you this morning, nor that I was with you in the tavern. This would have caused such a row. Here are the ins and outs of jealousy."

As Chopin became intrigued with Sand, he confided in Grzymała. Among his first impressions was that he found her "disagreeable," but that turned into infatuation. From the end of October 1836 through the fall and winter, Chopin and Sand attended the same soirées and musical affairs, but he was still wrapped up in the hope that he might marry Maria Wodzińska. By August of that year, the hope had all but disappeared. Sand invited him to Nohant a few times in the spring of 1837, but he refused. In April of that year, Chopin had to cancel his plans to perform at the Salle Érard with, among others, Liszt. Illness was the reason. It wasn't until October of 1837—about a year after their first meeting—that Sand and Chopin began to see each other more regularly, and it was in May of 1838 that she asked Grzymała what a relationship with Chopin would mean. She was still romantically involved with Félicien Mallefille, her children's tutor, and she seemed unwilling to sever ties with him. In a letter to Grzymała, she says, "I have already taken into my hands the fate of another [meaning Mallefille], and therefore would not be able to replace that which he discarded for me." Instead of confronting this problem head-on, she left Mallefille in Nohant with the children, and returned to Paris.

By late summer 1838, Sand's close friend, the painter Eugène Delacroix, was sketching a joint portrait of Chopin and Sand; this is perhaps as good an indication as any of their couplehood. By September, she was writing to Delacroix about her happiness: "I am beginning to believe that angels can appear disguised as men, dwelling for some time upon the earth. . . . If in one hour's time God were to send me to death, I would not complain, as three months have passed in undisturbed intoxication." Even Mallefille seemed all right with things, publishing a favorable review of Chopin and his *Polish Ballade*. This generous mood would not last, and soon, Mallefille challenged Chopin to a duel over Sand.

Sand and her children set off for a winter in Mallorca, and Chopin followed them a little more than a week after their departure. They enjoyed a few weeks of ease and happiness prior to Chopin's grave illness (see chapter 9). Sand biographer André Maurois surmised that Fryderyk and George shared a physical relationship only briefly. In his interpretation, Chopin seemed burdened by Sand's attempts at seduction. After his recovery from the illness that overtook him in Mallorca, she finally understood that Chopin could not indulge in any physical pleasures with her. Maurois said "[Chopin] was not made for pleasures of love. Always ill, he could not stand them, and despite her supplications, 'Aurora' very soon adopted a moderation that subsequently became total abstention."

Back in Nohant sometime later, she carved the date of June 19, 1839, into the wood panel next to a window in her bedroom. We don't know precisely what this date signifies, but there are two theories that have proven stubborn survivors, yet both entirely guesses. First, this date might have been Sand and Chopin's anniversary of the first time they had sex. Or perhaps this is the date of the last time they had sex. Sand was not one for these kinds of memorials, and many of her detractors spoke of the free nature with which she began and ended physical relationships. Later on, she would intimate that she decided to not ask these kinds of acts from Chopin. It's unclear what the actual truth is, but we do know that after this date, Chopin's creative output would blossom, and some of his most celebrated works would find their genesis.

In her memoir, which she wrote many years after Chopin's death, she described his sometimes mercurial moods: "Alive for an instant to sweet affection and the smiles of destiny, he was afflicted for days, for weeks, by the crassness of an indifferent listener or the vexations of daily life. And strange to say, a great cause for sorrow did not grieve him so much as a little one." In many ways, his "magnificent inconsistencies" were vexing to her, and yet, she could not or would not let him go. Because she was the more prolific writer, we have more of her thoughts on the matter of their relationship than we have of his. Sand, who seemed always interested in "protecting weaker beings," as one of her biographers has said, found something irresistible in Chopin. In many ways, he was emotionally unavailable to her, and yet she pursued him. She called him "little one" and may have come to see him more as a child than a fully grown adult. He did not offer her emotional support as she did him, and it was her desire to deny him the opportunity, reasoning, "He had plenty of ills of his own to bear. Mine would have broken his back, and therefore he knew little about them, and understood less." She tried to balance care of him with care of her own children, sometimes failing to maintain that balance. There appears to be genuine care and concern for Chopin and of course for her children, but perhaps also a stubborn yet impossible desire to be all things to all people.

When their affair began to break apart, it was Grzymała who was the intermediary. He had helped them with all kinds of practical matters—renting apartments and furniture—and then was caught in the middle of their rupture. What caused it seems to be a few things: familial disagreements including those with Maurice, Solange, and Solange's fiancée and then husband, the sculptor Clésinger; Chopin's worsening health did not help matters. Sand was reaching the end of her ability to continue to care for him. In May of 1847, Sand wrote to Pierre Hetzel that she was relieved to have seen Chopin through his latest illness, "but every attack worsens his state of health, and from that perspective my future looks bleak." She also wrote to Grzymała of her despair: "For seven years I have lived with him like a virgin. . . . I know that many people accuse me . . . that I have ruined him with my tempestuous sensuality . . . he complains that I have ruined him with my lack of tenderness."

By the summer of 1847, Chopin's desire to help Solange infuriated Sand. This is what ended up finally causing them to part ways. Although the break was wrenching for Sand—especially because it was with her own daughter as well as her former lover—there was an element of relief in it. She wrote to a friend, "I can finally begin a new life." To Chopin, she bid him farewell, and asked him to take care of Solange, "since, in your opinion, it is she to whom you should devote yourself. . . . Farewell, my friend. . . . I shall thank God for this peculiar conclusion to nine years of devoted friendship." Their last meeting was by chance in March of 1848. Chopin told Sand that Solange had given birth to a child. Their conversation was pleasant, if superficial.

Chopin would live just one more year, and Sand would live decades longer. Grzymała, mutual friend of the couple, who was one of the few with Chopin as he was dying, formed the opinion that the relationship with Sand might have been detrimental. He wrote about Chopin's final days, speaking of his "death struggle." "At such moments," he wrote, "my mind was crushed by the thought that if he had not the ill luck to know G. Sand, who poisoned his whole life, he might have lived to be as old as Cherubini." Perhaps this is an exaggeration, born of grief, or perhaps this was a true assessment of the unhealthy relationship Grzymała witnessed. In either case, the relationship between Sand and Chopin was, like any love relationship, replete with both good times and hard times. In their case, other factors seemed to have added complications: their unique needs as creators of art; familial issues with Sand's children; his chronic illness; her need to caretake. They remained companions for nearly a decade, but their relationship ended as these things do. One might argue that the biggest tragedy of all was the lack of reconciliation at the end, but it seemed they just ran out of time.

BALLADES

One of the genres that Chopin undertook in those first few precious years with Sand as his companion was the ballade. The name ballade has many old associations, including the Italian Renaissance *ballate* or the eponymous old French poetic form. Chopin's ballades may have been inspired by the poetry of Adam Mickiewicz, who is considered Poland's greatest national poet. We have no concrete associations, however, and can only guess at what Chopin intended to evoke with the word. Certainly, using "ballade" to name a piano work allows a connection to literature, even if that connection is vague and unspecific. There is no discernible narrative intended, but we may create one as we listen, perceiving shapes and events in the notes and phrases.

Chopin composed four ballades for solo piano between 1835 and 1842. They represent Chopin's efforts to expand and give weight to solo piano works by infusing them with some of the formal methods found in larger scale works like the symphony and the concerto. This means that harmonic concerns shape the form, and in the words of Jim Samson, a specialist on Chopin's ballades, "variation and transformation are seminal structures." Structurally, the ballades follow a form that is similar to sonata form, but with some variations. Indeed, we may argue that there is no "perfect" rendering of any form, and that every version must be seen in relation to the other "imperfect" renderings. Generally speaking, sonata form, which is often found in the opening movements of symphonies, sonatas, string quartets, and concertos (there are some specific alterations for concertos), presents two themes—usually in differing keys—at the beginning. After a developmental middle section, the two themes return, this time in the same key. Chopin did not merely use this form as given; he also made significant, if sometimes subtle changes. In discussing the works and their structural basis, one scholar has suggested that Chopin found the "hidden sideroads branching off" the established forms. Chopin's Ballades and the innovations therein inspired other composers, like Franz Liszt, and Johannes Brahms.

Chopin composed the First Ballade in the 1830s, although it is uncertain when exactly he first sketched out ideas for the work. Varying sources, some unreliable, aver that it was begun in 1831, but stylistic and paper evidence suggest its genesis came a few years later. Nevertheless, the work was published in the summer of 1836 and given opus number 23. He dedicated the work to Baron Nathaniel von Stockhausen, ambassador to France. After a seven-measure introduction, Chopin presents two themes. The opening theme in a lilting 6/4 meter and G minor tonality carries the sense of longing or yearning. Chopin explores this melancholic theme for nearly forty measures before providing an energetic transition to the second theme. The second theme in E-flat major begins softly and gently, but is soon infiltrated by the first theme. A more passionate and fortissimo restatement of the second theme takes over, leading us into the developmental section. This centerpiece of development expands upon our original theme, but also provides a new waltz-like theme, providing contrast before our return to the original themes. Chopin subverts expectations by presenting the themes in reverse order than we might expect: theme two is followed by theme one. There is a passionate coda, finally shaking off lyricism for a bravura display.

The dramatic nature of this Ballade has made it a favorite for films. It is this Ballade—especially the second theme—that forms something of a musical soundpost for the relationship of Sand and Chopin in the film *Impromptu*. The work also appears in Roman Polanski's film *The Pianist*. Adrien Brody as Władysław Szpilman plays the melancholy first theme and the coda for a sympathetic German officer (see chapter 4). The Ballade also makes an appearance in a 1991 symphony by Polish-Jewish composer Mieczysław Weinberg. His Symphony No. 21, subtitled "Kaddish," was dedicated to those who died in the Warsaw Ghetto. Chopin's music is quoted in the elegiac first movement. The piano presents just two measures of the ballade (the G minor theme) before being interrupted.

Chopin first made reference to the Second Ballade, op. 38, in a letter he sent to Julian Fontana from Mallorca. The letter dates from mid-December, about three weeks after Chopin had his first health crisis on the island. He held out hope of productivity despite his illness and despite still waiting for delivery of a piano. "I think I shall soon send you my Preludes and a Ballade. Go to [Auguste] Léo. Don't say that I'm ill; they'd get a thousandfold scare. And to Pleyel." Various references follow, over the course of a few months. In August of the following year, Chopin asked to have the fair copy back to make changes. Differences between what we might call the "original" version and the edited version became a fascination for composer Camille Saint-Saëns (1835–1921), who analyzed the changes in an essay called "A Chopin Manuscript: the F major Ballade in the Making." That there were such notable revisions is an intriguing window into the compositional process of Chopin, and shines a light on what an exacting perfectionist he could be. Although, it is actually quite amusing to note that the title page that exists—in Chopin's own hand—carries a rather glaring error that was not corrected: a misspelling of the dedicatee's name. Robert Schumann had dedicated his eight-movement piano solo, *Kreisleriana* op. 16, to Chopin, and Chopin returned the favor with Ballade No. 2, but signaled his lack of attention to his contemporary by spelling his name "Schuhmann."

The work was composed over three years, from 1836 to 1839. There appears to be a thematic relationship between this Ballade's main theme and the G major Nocturne, op. 37, no. 2; the two works were composed around the same time. The opening theme is a lovely *siciliano* melody, folk-like and unassuming. The second theme provides contrast in almost every way. It is fiery, quick, and *fortissimo*, and yet Chopin briefly sneaks in the *siciliano* rhythm as the initial fire dies away. The first theme returns, transitioning again—but without interruption—into the tempestuous A minor theme. There is a traditional reading of this Ballade that suggests corruption and loss of innocence, with the folk-like melody standing in for purity, and the A minor theme conflicting with it in an almost violent way. Of course, Chopin made no explicit connection himself, and many of these works are seen through the eyes of listeners who may crave an answer to the question, "What does it mean?"

Ballade No. 3, op. 47 was composed in 1841 and was dedicated to Pauline de Noailles. There is a hopeful mood to this Ballade, underlined by the opening of the piece, which is uncomplicated and sweet. In this work, we observe Chopin taking more of those side roads away from established forms, and these deviations can be interpreted in many ways. Some commentators discern the shape of a rondo in Chopin's revisits of the themes, while Samson sees a "blending" of formal functions normally found in sonata form. Chopin gives us two themes, but they are thematically related in a way unseen in the previous two Ballades. Some interpretations hold that the themes are so similar as to constitute a monothematic work. It may be, in this case, that the formal analysis fails to illuminate anything significant to enhance our appreciation. Suffice it to say the work is almost uniformly lighthearted throughout, with only occasional hints at more serious underpinnings. This lack of overwrought drama has led some to link this work, and indeed Chopin's steady output of music, to the stability he had found with Sand and the favorable working conditions at Nohant. Chopin and Sand had spent a peaceful summer at her family's retreat, and Chopin's productivity in 1841 reached its peak.

The final Ballade was composed in 1842, and was dedicated to Baroness Rothschild, a woman who introduced Chopin to important members of the Parisian aristocracy. We see a further blending of functional forms in this work, here sonata form and variation form. In terms of level of difficulty, this Ballade seems to be the most challenging to play. It is the Ballade that relies most heavily on counterpoint, and Chopin's displays of virtuosity show a degree of artfulness and commitment to the overall character of the work. That is to say, nowhere does one feel that virtuosity is there simply for its own sake. Chopin achieves a sublimity with this melancholy Ballade that, in retrospect, shines as the summit of his expressive powers. It displays inventive thematic transformation and variations, and ends with an intricately complex coda that shows off Chopin's mastery of counterpoint. This work is highly dramatic, melancholy, and full of passion. To see this work in historical context, it may be an apt comparison to see this Ballade as functioning in the same way as an elided cadence functions in music: it is both the end of something and the beginning of something else. In this case, the Ballade closes the chapter on this genre and Chopin's struggle to establish himself, and opens the chapter of Chopin's final years of composing and the apex of his unique and singular style.

7

CHOPIN AND THE VOICE

We don't think of Chopin as a composer of vocal music, yet write songs he did. As they are something of an anomaly in his output, they are often omitted from discussions about Chopin's works, but Chopin had a deep reverence for the human voice and he was a passionate fan of opera. One of Chopin's favorite voices belonged to his close friend, Delfina Potocka, whose presence in his life brought joy and consistency. Chopin's songs are delicate treasures, even if they do not reflect the highest complexity of his art. Along with an exploration of these songs, we must discuss the Polish poets who provided the poetry for them. Some of the songs had second lives as piano transcriptions and other arrangements.

THE OPERATIC IN CHOPIN'S MUSIC

Chopin's name and his legacy are virtually inseparable from the piano. His own artistic ambitions found their alpha and omega on the keyboard, and there was little to entice him elsewhere. His few orchestral pieces are evidence enough of this. But the absence of substantial vocal works—especially opera—from his oeuvre doesn't provide an accurate picture of his passions. As an aficionado, Chopin showed great interest in not only the voice but the violin as well, yet he paid little attention to either as a composer. He was fortunate enough to have been raised in Warsaw, where he could be exposed to performances by Europe's most popular touring musicians and read about cultural happenings abroad in more than a dozen literary journals and a weekly music publication. Niccolò Paganini came to play in Warsaw and Chopin saw him there. He was also pleased to see Paganini again in Paris in 1831. By 1834, friend Mendelssohn was comparing Chopin's works on piano with Paganini's work on the violin, but never would Chopin write music for the solo violin, no matter how much it moved him.

It was similar with the voice. While still in Warsaw, he was privileged enough to hear the singers Angelica Catalani and Henriette Sonntag. So impressed was he with the latter, he reportedly attended all eleven concerts she gave in that city. We know from correspondence and other contemporary accounts some of the pieces he heard and performances he attended. We know that he saw Handel's *Messiah* in Berlin as well as Domenico Cimarosa's opera, *Il matrimonio segreto*. During his first years in Paris, Chopin almost nightly availed himself of the three opera houses close to where he lived. The Royal Academy of Music, also known as the Paris Opera, was the closest to Chopin's apartment. There he heard Adolphe Nourrit and Laura Cinti-Damoreau. Also nearby was the Théâtre des Italiens, which put on Italian opera led by Rossini often featuring the vocal talent of some of the world's greatest singers, including Giuditta Pasta, Giovanni Rubini, and María Malibrán. And finally, the furthest away, but still only a short carriage ride, was the Opéra-Comique. Chopin was particularly fond of the offerings at the Italian opera house, although he was known to frequent the Café Feydeau—across from the Opéra-Comique—or the Café du Divan, across from the Royal Academy, for late night drinks.

Singing was something of an ideal for him. He often recommended that his students go to the opera to listen to the way singing voices interpreted phrases. "Singing" to him was a way to explain how to play. If one might speculate on the implications of this, we must remember two important things about the piano. First, its very nature is percussive, as a hammer hits a string to produce the sound. This can be done softly or loudly, but no matter what, the percussion must still occur to get sound. Second, the piano requires no breath to play, so phrasing will be challenging to teach. Other instruments, like the flute for example, require the player to choose when to breathe to make the best of a phrase. Likewise, a singer must choose to breathe in places that make sense in the music. One mustn't breathe in the middle of a word, for example. Ideally, the breath will match with the phrase. Pianists don't have to make choices based on when they must breathe, but for the purposes of interpretation, it is essential that they think in some equivalent way. Perhaps this is what Chopin was getting at with his emphasis on singing as a model for his students. Perhaps he was looking for a way to illustrate this connection within each phrase. Singers and other wind instrumentalists experience this *legato* phrasing as part of the breath. Even string players think in terms of bow direction. Proper expression on the piano, then, requires some forethought.

In Paris in the first half of the nineteenth century, it seemed to many that the fast track to fame and fortune was by writing opera. Of course Chopin's friends wanted to see his star rise as quickly as possible, but Chopin had other ideas. Furthermore, there were those who felt it was Chopin's duty as a patriotic Pole to write a nationalistic opera in Polish. Among the loudest voices advocating for this were poets who likely wanted to write a libretto for Chopin to set to music. Poet Stefan Witwicki was particularly supportive of the idea. Such an undertaking was also suggested by Józef Elsner, one of Chopin's first teachers. Chopin, although quite polite in most circumstances, knew his own mind. He also knew it was a difficult road, even with connections. Chopin noted that Meyerbeer, who had been a successful opera composer for a decade, waited for three years until a production of *Robert le diable* was premiered. What chance might someone have to get his first opera produced in Paris, especially a Polish nationalist opera? Finally, and probably most importantly, he did not believe that opera was for him, and he was not to be swayed on the point. In late 1831, he wrote to Elsner, explaining that he was going to "[clear] a path for myself in the world as a pianist, putting off till some later time those higher artistic hopes which your letter rightly puts forward."

Opera was not in the cards for Chopin, but he did try his hand at songs for voice and piano. Chopin's first exploration of song was bound up with his first infatuation, Konstancja Gładkowska, a singer. Another one of his songs found its way into the album of a woman Chopin thought he might marry, Maria Wodzińska. The songs are certainly not as well-known as his pieces for solo piano, and they are not often performed, but they are endlessly charming and show off a talent for vocal writing that we can otherwise discern in his melodic, lyrical phrases for piano. In looking at Chopin's instrumental work we can hear vocal influences in certain pieces, especially the nocturnes. More than one of Chopin's contemporaries noted the influence of bel canto in those pieces. In his book *The Romantic Generation*, Charles Rosen saw Chopin's Etude no. 7 in C-sharp minor, op. 25, as being thematically linked to a scene from Bellini's opera, *Norma*.

DELFINA POTOCKA

One of Chopin's favorite voices belonged to his close friend, Delfina Potocka. A Polish countess and musician, she was one of the chosen few gathered at Chopin's deathbed during his final hours. The two had met in Paris when they were in their early twenties, Potocka becoming first a student and then a confidant. She was born Delfina Komar in what is now Ukraine in 1807. She gained her title by marrying Count Mieczysław Potocki in 1825. The marriage produced two daughters, but ended in divorce. Potocka then traveled abroad where she made the acquaintance of Chopin and other artists, including the Polish poet Zygmunt Krasiński, with whom she had a long romantic relationship.

Countess Potocka had a reputation among her Parisian friends as something of a sexual libertine. Chopin's friend Delacroix called her "the enchantress" and said of her: "[I] thought that I had never met with anything more perfect." Krasiński himself described his lover as a woman in whose soul were "smoldering fires that become volcanic expressions." There is an oft-quoted line from Krasiński joking that she was "Don Juan in petticoats," which seems to point to her alleged promiscuity, but the full quote is actually more revealing. The full quote alludes to an undercurrent of dissatisfaction, even melancholy. Krasiński said that once her smoldering fires die out, "she becomes unbearably capricious . . . obsessed with the need to joke so that she may escape the boredom which gnaws at her. Then she is a pampered child, or Don Juan in petticoats, who has experienced everything and now cries, 'Give me the moon—I want to find out if it tastes like good marzipan.'"

There are rumors that she and Chopin were lovers, but there is no hard evidence to that effect. Even if we are to allow that something *had* happened between them, it seems that it caused no drama and meant nothing beyond friendship to either of them. Potocka arrived in Chopin's life before George Sand and she remained after Sand's exit from Chopin's life.

Rumors, however, are stubborn things that grow exponentially in the absence of evidence. In the 1940s, a Polish woman (called either a musicologist or an amateur musicologist) named Paulina Czernicka alleged that she had come into some correspondence between Chopin and Potocka, with whom she claimed to be related. The contents of these letters set forth a romantic history between Chopin and Potocka, and included innuendo-filled sexual descriptions. These letters were declared to be forgeries, but numerous books about Chopin dutifully included them as part of the documentary evidence of his life. Furthermore, a film was released in 1999, drawing upon these forged letters as the basis for a narrative. Director Tony Palmer's film, *The Strange Case of Delfina Potocka*, dramatizes the romantic relationship between Chopin and Potocka, and offers little in the way of historical accuracy. Palmer, whose career as a director spans both stage and screen, cast the same actress (Penelope Wilton) to play both Delfina and Paulina, who the film says is Delfina's granddaughter. There are no facts to be gleaned here, although it is an interesting case study of how sensational ideas continue, if the subject matter is salacious enough.

The overwhelming evidence from Chopin's authentic correspondence and accounts from his contemporaries paint a picture of a certain kind of man. In describing the Chopin "revealed" in these forged letters, Arthur Hedly says that this false Chopin "had, in fact, achieved miracles of successful hypocrisy and had completely outwitted the penetrating feminine gaze of George Sand, the delicate perception of Delacroix and the keen glance of Berlioz."

The history of these letters is this: Paulina Czernicka brought the letters to a Professor Szpinalski in 1941, and a few years later to the Chopin Institute in Warsaw. Perhaps "letters" is the wrong word here, as they consisted of fragments, copied over. The band of Polish musicologists who were ready to put their skepticism aside and treat the originals with archival respect received only excerpts, paragraphs, a sentence, with the declaration that the originals had been "destroyed." Although there was some similarity to Chopin's writing style, there were also "exaggerations, flaws and inconsistencies which [could not] stand up to critical examination." Take, for example, how he referred to his long-time partner, George Sand. In his proven correspondence he referred to her to others as "Mme Sand," or "George." (The latter was much less common.) In the alleged letters, he calls her "Aurora" or "Sandowa." Furthermore, any reader of Chopin's correspondence will note how much he chats about the people, places, and things around him, and not greater philosophical themes. In fact, in the correspondence, there is precious little about his compositional process, or even his thoughts on pieces he had written. Yet, in the Potocka letters, he is primarily concerned with the way he views composition, and takes this one step further by connecting his level of creativity with his level of sexual activity. That is to say, the false Chopin of these letters seems to think that engaging in sexual acts with a woman saps his creative force. Among the more graphic of the alleged letters, we have Chopin writing to the Countess worrying over the loss of his creative force through sex: "Think how much of that precious fluid and strength I have lost, ramming you to no purpose, since I have not given you a baby: and God knows how many of my finest inspirations and musical thoughts have been lost forever."

Further study of the documents reveals a Chopin strangely prescient about people and events, pointing to the fact that they were written not in the time they supposedly took place, but from the present with an eye on the past. After careful study and indeed the efforts of an entire conference full of scholars, the musicologists and linguists at the Chopin Institute in Warsaw released a letter from their president. He called the letters "spurious" and went on to explain some of the problems, including anachronistic linguistic expressions in the text. Czernicka's allegations that she came into the letters as a familial descendant of Delfina Potocka were also called into question as it was discovered that Czernicka might have had a connection to a different branch of the Komar family, one without a coat of arms. The president also declared that Potocka herself entrusted the entirety of her correspondence to a friend, Mme. Alexandrina Tyszkiewicz, who said that there were, in fact, no letters from Chopin in the collection. Czernicka tragically committed suicide in 1949; one uncorroborated source claimed she ended her own life at that time to coincide with the hundredth anniversary of Chopin's death.

The real Delfina Potocka and the real Chopin were definitely close friends. Chopin dedicated two pieces of music to her. To some, that alone is proof that there was no romantic connection; Chopin dedicated no music at all to George Sand, his companion of a decade. There were also no pieces dedicated to Konstancja Gładkowska (his teenage infatuation) or Maria Wodzińska (whom he thought he might marry). Arthur Hedley suggests that the reason for this was Chopin's intensely private nature. Perhaps he didn't want people to read too much into his feelings for these ladies.

Chopin dedicated the Parisian edition of the Piano Concerto No. 2 to Delfina Potocka. She is also the dedicatee of one of Chopin's most famous pieces. In the summer of 1846, a time when Chopin seemed to be enjoying good health and emotional stability, he composed a trio of sprightly waltzes. One of them is said to have been inspired by a playful little dog named Marquis, who lived with Chopin and George Sand. In one version of the story, the dog was chasing his tail; in another, he was playing with a ball of wool. Whatever the true story, Chopin composed the "Minute" Waltz, which was informally called *Valse au petit chien* (*Little Dog Waltz*) supposedly based on Marquis's scampering.

At one point, near the end of his life, he wrote the words "Nella Miseria" ("In Misery") in Potocka's album. Chopin was making reference to a quote from Dante's *The Divine Comedy*, which reads, "Nessun maggior dolore che ricordarsi del tempo felice nella miseria . . ." ("No greater sorrow than to recall the happy times in misery"). He had made good memories with her, and their friendship was destined to be cut short by his illness. Countess Potocka arrived at Chopin's on October 16, 1849, the day before he died. On this, his penultimate day, Chopin requested that Delfina sing a bit for him. She did, accompanying herself at the piano, singing through her tears, until Chopin was overwhelmed and asked her to stop. Although we are not fully certain of what she sang, many accounts say *Dignare O Domine* from Handel's *Te Deum*, the text of which says, in essence: "O Lord, keep us from sin today/ Have mercy on us/ Do not let us be confounded/ O Lord, in thee I have hoped, do not abandon me."

THE POLISH POETS AND CHOPIN'S SONGS

Fellow composer and contemporary of Chopin Robert Schumann once dismissed the genre of the art song as frivolous—until he fell in love with the woman who would become his devoted wife. He subsequently composed nearly a hundred songs in a single year. Chopin, whose early romantic feelings may have caused a similar awakening, turned to the genre of the art song when he was about nineteen years old. It was around that time that he began to notice a young mezzo soprano by the name of Konstancja Gładkowska. It was also around the time that Chopin was spending long hours at a coffeehouse called Dziurka (The Keyhole). It was through the circle of young artists and activists who discussed politics and shared ideas at Dziurka that Chopin made the acquaintance of poet Stefan Witwicki. When his thoughts turned to writing songs in 1829–1830, Chopin set seven poems by Stefan Witwicki in the first batch. Witwicki ultimately provided the text for ten of Chopin's songs. He was also the dedicatee of a set of Chopin's mazurkas. When Chopin moved to Paris in 1831, Witwicki followed him a year later. There the two met up again, this time joined by a third Polish ex-patriot (and another poet), Adam Mickiewicz. Chopin had known of Mickiewicz's work, and had bought an edition of the poet's *Ballades and Romances* when he was still a teenager in Warsaw. (Mickiewicz's *Ballades and Romances* seem also to have inspired Chopin's ballades.)

Mickiewicz was born in 1798. He is considered one of the founders of Polish Romanticism. Mickiewicz and two others—Juliusz Słowacki and Zygmunt Krasiński (Delfina Potocka's lover)—are considered the "Three Bards" of Polish Romanticism. The term in Polish is *Trzej Wieszcze*, which means "three prophets" or "three seers." The name refers to the thought that the three were writing ideas pertaining to the future of Poland. Each one brought something unique to the collective, with Krasiński the one most often thought of as a prophet of Poland's future. Mickiewicz's lyric poetry represented the present, while Słowacki was the romantic poet and dramatist. Zygmunt Krasiński provided the text for one of Chopin's songs, while Mickiewicz provided two.

Before his years in Paris, Mickiewicz had been exiled to Russia for his political activities and spent five years there. He found a home in literary circles in both St. Petersburg and Moscow, and continued to write. He gained enough favor with his many contacts there that he was eventually allowed to leave. He traveled to Berlin and Prague, and followed those journeys with a visit to Italy. After that, he moved to Geneva, where he made the acquaintance of Krasiński. It is thought that he might have been involved with transmitting political information between the Italian and the French. He settled in Paris in 1832, finding a thriving Polish émigré community. Among Mickiewicz's most important works is the epic poem *Pan Tadeusz*, which he published in 1834. Mickiewicz knew fellow writer George Sand in Paris before she and Chopin became companions. Eventually, Mickiewicz was appointed to a position at the Collège de France. He was a popular lecturer, and Sand and Chopin often attended his lectures. Always showing special concern for his fellow émigrés, Chopin felt that the available translation of Mickiewicz's drama *Dziady* (*Forefather's Eve*) did not do the original work justice. At one point, he encouraged Mickiewicz and Sand to collaborate on a new version, but it did not come to pass. Chopin and Mickiewicz remained friends through the years. Near the end of Chopin's life, when he returned to Paris after his final London visit, his health was failing. He tried to soldier on, beginning sketches for what would be his final mazurka. He even visited with Mickiewicz, and played piano for the poet, who was going through his own difficulties. Mickiewicz's troubles were related to marriage and career, not health, but the two did their best to comfort each other.

Composers of song in the Romantic period had so much wonderful, heartfelt poetry from which to choose. Composers like Schumann and Franz Schubert, for example, were setting the very finest German poetry. Chopin could have done likewise, but instead, he chose to set Polish texts, largely taken from poets he knew personally. In 1829, Chopin began his song journey with Witwicki's texts *Życzenie* (*The Wish* or *A Maiden's Wish*) and *Gdzie lubi* (*What She Likes* or *A Fickle Maid*); and *Jakież kwiaty* (*Which Flowers*) by I. Maciejowski. Thoughts of Konstancja Gładkowska's mezzo soprano voice might have been on Chopin's mind as he wrote these songs; the ranges of each sit very comfortably in the mezzo register. In 1830, he composed four more texts by Witwicki: *Wojak* (*The Warrior* or *Before the Battle*), *Hulanka* (*Merrymaking* or *Drinking Song*), *Poseł* (*The Messenger*), and *Czary* (*Enchantment* or *Witchcraft*). He also set the first of two texts by Mickiewicz, *Precz z moich oczu!* (*Out of My Sight* or *Remembrance*).

Chopin, however, did not have personal experiences with all of the poets. In 1830 or 1831, he set Ludwik Osiński's Polish translation of a traditional Lithuanian folk song, *Pionska litewska* (*A Lithuanian Song*), but seems not to have ever met the man. Chopin left Poland on November 2, 1830, and he arrived in Paris ten months later. During this time of transition, he still composed. Sometime in 1831 he wrote settings of two Witwicki texts: *Smutna rzeka* (*Troubled Waters* or *The Sad Stream*) and *Narzeczony* (*The Bridegroom's Return* or *The Return Home*). For the five subsequent years, Chopin's focus shifted away from this genre; his presence as a pianist in Paris necessitated his work on solo piano pieces. His return to the art song came just as he began a relationship of sorts with Maria Wodzińska, a woman that he might have married, had circumstances been slightly different. At the end of the story, however, the only ring he gave her was a setting of *Pierścień* (*The Ring*), another Witwicki text. He wrote this song into her album the last time they were together.

In 1836, he set a text by poet Wincenty Pol called *Śpiew z mogiły* (*Leaves are Falling* or *Poland's Dirge*). This was a text that had nothing to do with romantic love, but was more a reflection of love for one's homeland when in exile. Pol was born in 1807 and was politically active during the November Uprising in 1830–1831. Like Mickiewicz and Witwicki, Pol was an important voice of Polish Romanticism. In his poem *Pieśń o ziemi naszej* (*Song of Our Land*), he outlined some of the main areas and customs of Poland. He was so involved with the details of Poland's geography, he was something of an armchair expert on the subject. His political experiences were covered in *Songs of Janusz*. Reportedly, Chopin was inspired by this work to write a dozen songs, of which *Śpiew z mogiły* would be the only surviving setting.

The following year, Chopin set *Moja pieszczotka* (*My Darling*), the other Mickiewicz text. In 1838, he set the tenth and final text by Witwicki, called *Wiosna* (*Spring*). Chopin turned to texts by Józef Bohdan Zaleski and Zygmunt Krasiński for his final surviving songs. He set Zaleski's *Dumka* (*Reverie* or *Mist Before My Eyes*) in 1840, *Śliczny chłopiec* (*Handsome Lad*) in 1841, and *Niema czego trzeba* (*I Want What I Have Not* or *Faded and Vanished*) in 1845, which is actually an embellished version of the music Chopin used for *Dumka*. Also in 1845, Chopin set Zaleski's *Dwojaki koniec* (*The Double End* or *The Two Corpses*). He set Krasiński's *Melodia* (*Melody* or *Lament*) in 1847. A few songs mentioned in correspondence after Chopin's death have never turned up. Julian Fontana, for example, wrote to Chopin's sister Ludwika about a song called *Płótno* (*Linen*) in 1852. In that same year, Scottish pupil and friend, Jane Stirling, wrote about three unnamed songs in a letter to Ludwika. There were also about a half a dozen songs attributed to Chopin that were spurious. In the final tally, we have nineteen surviving songs: ten with texts by Witwicki, four by Zaleski, two by Mickiewicz, and one each from Krasiński, Pol, and Osiński.

Chopin composed songs beginning in 1829, when he was still a teenager, although his style—throughout his exploration of the genre—is more akin to that of Franz Schubert (1797–1828), who wrote his Lieder a generation earlier. In general, the writing style isn't heavily chromatic, as one might expect, but rather quite tuneful with chromatic alterations that reflect early Romanticism. Perhaps Chopin merely felt less adventurous in song territory. The surviving songs were composed at various times during Chopin's thirty-nine years. Only two were published while Chopin was alive. In 1857, the composer's friend and musical executor Julian Fontana published op. 74, a set of sixteen songs. (The order of the set does not reflect the order in which the pieces were written.) Fontana published a seventeenth song separately, but it is now usually listed as part of op. 74. The final surviving two songs were published in 1910.

A few of Chopin's songs are through composed, but many of them display a strophic structure and hallmarks of some Polish folk song or dance influence. This was yet another way for Chopin to show his nationalistic feelings toward his homeland and nostalgia for the life and culture he left behind. Unlike his contemporary Schumann, who also wrote songs for voice and piano, Chopin's piano parts for his songs are more accompanimental, and less integrated into the dramatic narrative. We might expect that the piano parts of Chopin's songs would be complex and challenging, but the composer was sensitive to the voice, allowing it to be the focus. The vocal parts in some songs show effervescent joy while others demonstrate deep emotion and pathos.

Between the years of 1847 and 1860, Franz Liszt chose half a dozen of the songs from op. 74 and arranged them for piano solo, calling them 6 *Chants polonais*. He opens the set with *Życzenie*, followed by *Wiosna*. The third and fourth songs—*Pierścień* and *Hulanka*—are written to be played without a break between them. Liszt also includes a six-measure reprise of *Pierścień* before the coda of *Hulanka* to tie the pair together thematically. After that, the two final songs are *Moja pieszczotka* and *Narzeczony*. Liszt also used the melody from *Życzenie* as the second part of his three-movement piano suite, *Glanes de Woronince* (*Harvest at Woronińce*). He composed this work in 1847 at the estate of Princess

Carolyne zu Sayn-Wittgenstein in Ukraine. The first and last works in this collection are *dumky* (one of Chopin's songs is also called *Dumka*), which are short pieces inspired by Ukrainian folk songs. Chopin self-borrowed for *Życzenie* his Nocturne in C-sharp minor, which was published posthumously. Chopin also arranged a version of *Wiosna* for solo piano, and called it *Andantino*. He arranged this piece numerous times, leaving behind five versions dated within the decade of 1838 to 1848.

8

MUSICAL INHERITANCE

A talent like Chopin's does not develop in a vacuum. It is nurtured by teachers, colored by influences, and shaped by circumstances. In this chapter we look at Chopin's influences, like his contemporary, the famed virtuoso violinist, Niccolò Paganini. Chopin also learned the music of earlier composers whose pieces he played as a young student, among them Wolfgang Mozart and J. S. Bach. Although Chopin's style was singular, we cannot discount the importance of these musical threads woven into the tapestry of Chopin's music. To this end, we discuss the Preludes, which had a connection to Bach's *Well-Tempered Clavier*, and Chopin's Variations on Mozart's melody from *Don Giovanni*, "La ci darem la mano." Finally, we consider the technology of the pianos available to Chopin, which allowed him considerable expressive range.

NICCOLÒ PAGANINI

When Chopin was a young man in Warsaw, he was fortunate to see many of Europe's best performers and composers on the concert stage. One artist, who made waves throughout Europe for his exceptional virtuosity on the violin, impressed the then nineteen-year-old Chopin when he played in that city. By the time Chopin heard him play in 1829, the name Niccolò Paganini had become synonymous with virtuosity. His 24 Caprices for Solo Violin, op. 1 captivated audiences and encapsulated the height of violin technique of his time. In his capacity as a fan of music—not as a composer or performer—Chopin admired both the human voice (mostly in the form of opera) and the violin. When Paganini passed through Paris in 1831, Chopin reportedly attended all ten concerts given by the virtuoso. Chopin and Paganini finally met six years later in Paris. Elise Peruzzi, a friend of Paganini who was a pupil of Chopin, arranged the meeting. Peruzzi wrote about the encounter in her memoirs, noting that the two virtuosos seemed to have an instant mutual understanding.

Paganini was a native of Genoa, and his childhood was quite unhappy. Forced to practice and play for many hours of the day, the violinist said his own father would refuse to feed him if he had not been "diligent enough." Paganini's father sought a suitable teacher for him, although that proved quite difficult, as by the age of twelve, he was already sight-reading concertos. He ended up studying with Ferdinando Paër, an opera composer who lived in Parma. By the age of fifteen, Paganini was touring northern Italy. He secured a post at the court of Elisa Bonaparte Baciocchi, Napoleon's sister, who ruled over the region of Lucca, where Paganini had been named the first violin of the republic. He played there for a while, but when Baciocchi became the Grand Duchess of Tuscany, Paganini resumed life as a touring musician. He finally achieved notoriety outside of Italy by the late 1820s.

Paganini's virtuosity was so legendary—even in his own time—that rumors swirled concerning a pact with the devil. He was also a well-known gambler and womanizer. On one occasion, he lost everything while gambling, including the Amati instrument he had been playing. The story goes that a French merchant and amateur violinist, Monsieur Livron, loaned Paganini a 1743 Guarneri violin for a performance. When Livron heard what it sounded like in Paganini's hands, he refused to take it back, making it a gift to the talented violinist. The Guarneri became one of Paganini's favorite instruments, and was bequeathed to the city of Genoa after Paganini's death. He nicknamed it the "cannon" because it was capable of an impressive dynamic range. Paganini also called it the *Guarneri del Gesu*.

Because of Chopin's facility on the piano, it was not uncommon for Paganini and Chopin to be mentioned in the same breath. After all, Paganini's gift to the world was a reimagining of the violin and its capabilities; Chopin would do something similar with the piano. In 1834

Chopin spent some time with fellow composers Ferdinand Hiller and Felix Mendelssohn. They converged at Mendelssohn's home in Düsseldorf, and besides convivial socializing, the three played music together. After their visit, Mendelssohn wrote to his mother, "[Chopin] astonishes with his innovations, as Paganini has done on the violin, and he introduces marvels that would seem almost impossible."

Paganini's 24 Caprices for Solo Violin was itself influenced by Baroque composer and violinist Pietro Locatelli's *L'arte del violino*, a set of twenty-four caprices written in 1733. Paganini makes musical reference to Locatelli's Caprices in his own set (he quotes Locatelli's seventh Caprice in his first). The influence of Paganini's 24 caprices seems to have crossed over into the piano music of the first half of the nineteenth century, inspiring Robert Schumann's *Sechs Konzert Etüdien nach Capricen von Paganini* of 1832 and *6 Konsert-Etüdien nach Capricen de Paganini* from the following year. Liszt also began writing his *Grandes Études de Paganini* in 1832, a set of virtuosic piano pieces that he ultimately finished revising almost two decades later. The original versions and slightly simplified final versions are virtuosic pieces that require the utmost skill to perform. For example, there are some passages that require the pianist to reach one or two notes wider than an octave—an exceptional distance unreachable by all but the biggest and most flexible of hands. Liszt based each of the six études in the set on a musical theme from Paganini's work. The fourth piece, for example, draws upon the music of the first Caprice from Paganini's set of twenty-four, while the finale is a theme and variations based on the last Caprice in Paganini's op. 1.

Although there is discussion that the music of Chopin's op. 10 Études (which the composer dedicated to Liszt) was also fruit of the tree of Paganini's influence, Chopin made no explicit connection. As a younger composer, however, Chopin wrote *Souvenir de Paganini*, a short set of variations on the "Carnival of Venice" tune. Unlike Liszt's homage, which focused on the conspicuous display of virtuosity, Chopin's remains somewhat restrained. One modern commentary on Chopin and this piece averred, "to be the fuse and not the firework was what ultimately set Chopin apart from other virtuosos of the day." Chopin was not one to inject difficulty for the sake of difficulty. Beautiful simplicity was always his goal, something he called the "crowning reward of art." Chopin's *Souvenir de Paganini* is barely four minutes long;

it begins with a simple statement of the "Carnival of Venice" tune, which is followed by four variations and a coda. The variations embellish the tune, sometimes with triplets, sometimes with arpeggios. In Chopin's piece the right hand goes further afield, ultimately playing descending passages from high in the piano's range. Yet the resulting piece is always somewhat quiet, occasionally providing us with crescendos that grow to a *forte* dynamic but soon return to a quiet *piano*, with the coda mostly *pianissimo*.

VOICES FROM THE PAST

Bach had been dead for sixty years and Mozart for nearly twenty when Chopin was born. His very first piano teacher, Wojciech Żywny, a Boehmian violinist, introduced the six-year-old Chopin to the music of J. S. Bach and Wolfgang Mozart. An early biographer of Chopin, Frederick Niecks, said,

> The supremely-loved and enthusiastically-admired Mozart and Bach, must have had a share in Chopin's development; but it cannot be said that they left a striking mark on his music, with regard to which, however, it has to be remembered that the degree of external resemblance does not always accurately indicate the degree of internal indebtedness.

In 1838, Chopin set off on a trip to Mallorca where he would meet George Sand. For this trip, Chopin packed just two musical scores with him for the entirety of the three-month trip: the two volumes of J. S. Bach's *Well-Tempered Clavier*. One can purchase a facsimile copy of Chopin's edition of the *Well-Tempered Clavier*, which features Chopin's editorial notes written in it. On this trip, Chopin worked on a project that was an homage of sorts to Bach's keyboard monument, a cycle of twenty-four preludes. J. S. Bach's music represents the pinnacle of the High Baroque period. It's full of strict counterpoint, yet also enjoys some of the most beautiful, delicate melodies, seemingly spun from the finest thread into intricate lace. Because Chopin sounds only like Chopin, his music does not at first invite comparisons with Bach's style, but as Jeremy Siepmann notes, "polyphonic textures pervade [Chopin's] music." But more than this, Chopin played a fugue a day: "as a daily exercise," and as Chopin biographer Tad Szulc likened it to a religious ritual: "a soul-saving religious obeisance." Chopin often told his pupils, "Practice Bach constantly."

Bach composed the first book of the *Well-Tempered Clavier* (*WTC*) in 1722 when he was working in Cöthen. (A second volume followed twenty years later.) He wrote Book I for students who were learning how to play, but especially for students who already possessed some skill. It is a methodical exploration of each key in the well-tempered tuning system. In this system, the twelve half-steps of the octave are tuned at a near-equal distance, resulting in a system where every key was said to sound in tune (our modern ears are used to so-called equal temperament, an even more precise division of the twelve half-steps). The meantone tuning of Bach's time made some keys sound different, and were consequently less desirable to composers. The well-tempered tuning system, therefore, allowed a composer to write in any of the possible keys. Bach composed a prelude and fugue for each of the twenty-four keys. Each prelude is freer in design, while the fugues are structured around strict imitation.

Although manuscript copies of the *WTC* were passed around musical circles, the work wasn't published formally until fifty years after the composer's death. Bach's style had been out of fashion for some time because the first Classical composers favored simpler melodies and less counterpoint, but composers like Haydn and Mozart carefully studied the *WTC* and gradually brought more complexity and counterpoint into Classical composition. Mozart went so far as to transcribe some of Bach's three- and four-part fugues for string trio. The advantage of such arrangements is that they allow us to hear how each voice behaves, something that is hard to distinguish when all of the "voices" are played on a single instrument by a single player. The complex structure of the fugue becomes more transparent as does Bach's genius for counterpoint.

From a pedagogical standpoint, using the music of Bach in keyboard lessons teaches all of the fingers to share a similar weight of touch. Chopin wanted his students to have facility of movement, and also be able to play complex textures while still bringing out important singular lines within the complexity.

Contemporary Robert Schumann described Chopin's preludes as an "intimate diary." Chopin had a special connection to the Baroque style, yet he is held up as a true Romantic. The term "prelude" suggests an opening piece that introduces perhaps a larger work that follows. In the realm of Romantic character pieces, the prelude was a stand-alone, one-movement work that could display a variety of moods. Chopin's preludes were short, none of them more than ninety measures long. The shortest of the collection was just twelve bars, leading some critics—including contemporary Robert Schumann—to view them as somehow incomplete, or mere sketches. Liszt, however, viewed them as innovative and poetic.

Chopin composed twenty-four preludes between 1835 and 1839 and collected them into one opus number (28), publishing them in 1839. In the French edition, Chopin dedicated the collection to Camille Pleyel, a piano-maker, and the man who commissioned the work. For the German publication, Chopin chose a different dedicatee, composer Joseph Christoph Kessler. Kessler and Chopin knew each other from Kessler's visit to Warsaw in 1829, and it was in that year that Kessler had dedicated a set of twenty-four preludes to Chopin.

Although each work can stand alone, some scholars have suggested that the collection is one large work with twenty-four pieces, citing motivic connections among the preludes, and even musical connections from the ends of some preludes to the beginnings of others. Chopin never played all twenty-four in a row in a public performance. In fact, he never played more than four in a single concert. The twenty-four preludes vary in character, tempo, and key, and in the set they seem, for the most part, to alternate slow and fast. The keys follow the pattern of the circle of fifths, with each major key preceding its relative minor. This pattern of circle of fifths as an organizational paradigm had been used by Joseph Christoph Kessler in his set of twenty-four preludes. (In contrast, Bach had arranged his preludes with each successive key a half step higher than the one previous.)

Although the music suggests non-musical ideas, or emotions, Chopin didn't give them evocative names, like Schumann and Liszt did for some of their pieces that were of a similar character. Hans von Bülow suggested some names for the preludes like "Reunion," "Tolling Bells," "The Polish Dancer," and "Raindrop." Of these names, only "Raindrop" seems to be widely used. The twentieth prelude in the set became the basis for variations by Rachmaninoff and twentieth-century Italian composer Ferruccio Busoni.

Chopin wrote three other preludes, not in this set. No. 25 (also catalogued as op. 45) was composed in 1841 and dedicated to Princess E. Czernicheff. No. 26 had actually been composed in the 1830s and bears the tempo marking *presto con leggierezza*. It was a gift for Liszt's student and pianist Pierre Wolff. The twenty-seventh prelude—which was left incomplete—has been called the "Devil's Trill" by musicologist Jeffrey Kallberg. Giuseppe Tartini, a composer whose music Chopin might have heard, composed a violin sonata called "The Devil's Trill." Kallberg "realized" the prelude from Chopin's incomplete sketches. The piece was played in public for the first time in 2002. Despite the excitement of having a "new" piece by Chopin, any reconstruction or realization of incomplete sketches—by any composer—will bring up questions of the composer's true intentions. This prelude is no exception.

When Chopin first showed talent as a young boy, his early successes prompted comparisons with the child prodigy, Mozart. Chopin admired the work of Mozart, showing particular fondness for Mozart's operas and for the *Requiem*. There are a few instances in which he played Mozart publicly: in February of 1846, he performed a Mozart piano trio at a public appearance in Paris, and during his 1848 visit to London, he played a Mozart piano duet with Julius Benedict. He did not, however, give his students assigned piano pieces from Mozart, even though he respected the music. The connection to Mozart seems more emotional than musical. In the summer of 1846, in the midst of difficulties composing, he asked a friend to send him the pocket-sized score of Mozart's *Requiem*. In the final hours of his life in 1849, it was this piece that Chopin requested be played at his funeral.

The year 1827 was a difficult one for Chopin. He struggled with some health issues, but worse yet, he lost his younger sister Emilia to tuberculosis. Even in the midst of tragedy, Chopin composed, writing his Variations of Mozart's "La ci darem la mano" from the opera *Don Giovanni*. He was just a young man of seventeen at the time, and his experience with writing for the orchestra was limited, but he was sufficiently inspired to work out these variations with the large ensemble.

In the context of the opera, "La ci darem la mano" is a duet that takes place in Act 1, Scene 3, after Don Giovanni interrupts the wedding of Zerlina and Masetto. Don Giovanni sends Masetto away and endeavors to seduce Zerlina. This duet shows off Mozart's great gift for melody and for crafting a musical scene that allows for the musical lines of the characters to intertwine as Zerlina's resolve to refuse Don Giovanni weakens. Premiered in 1829 (when he was visiting Vienna) and published in 1830, Chopin's piece caused quite a stir, with Robert Schumann declaring about Chopin, "Hats off, gentlemen—a genius!"

The piece begins with a lengthy introduction, after which the piano presents "La ci darem la mano" in a very straightforward fashion. The first variation, marked *Brillante*, is fast and lively, as its name suggests, and the second is even faster than the first. An orchestral tutti intervenes in between the end of one variation and the beginning of another, with individual voices of the orchestral instruments punctuating these breaks. Some Variations require the orchestra to provide sustained chords to support the harmony, while in others the instruments play a more active role. The Fifth Variation, in a minor key, provides some contrast and drama to a brilliant piece. According to Chopin, the enthusiastic audience applauded every variation of the melody. The coda, marked *Alla Polacca*, returns us to the glittering charm of the early variations. The piece ends in such spectacular fashion and displays virtuosity throughout.

Chopin was sometimes amazed at the meanings other people ascribed to his music. If Chopin felt his music was representing something—an emotion, a narrative, or an event—he was quite tight-lipped about it. To hear that his compositions might be interpreted by critics as having meaning was odd to him. He mentions such a thing happening in a review of these "La ci darem la mano" Variations. Of course, the opera provided some idea of what might be represented, but Chopin certainly never intended that the composition be read in such a manner. In a letter to his dear friend Tytus, he explains a review:

> A few days ago, I received . . . a ten-page review, in which, after an immense preface, he goes on to analyse them, measure by measure; saying that they are not Variations in the usual sense, but some kind of fantastic *tableaux*. About the 2nd *Variation* he said that Don Juan is running with Leporello; that in the 3rd he is embracing Zerlina and Mazetto raging in the left hand; that in the 5th measure of the Adagio Don Juan is kissing Zerlina in D flat major. . . . One can die of the imagination of this German.

The review Chopin refers to in this letter is not the one from Robert Schumann, but rather from Schumann's teacher and future father-in-law, Friedrich Wieck. The review was published in two German musical journals, *Caecilia* and *Der Komet*. Chopin did not like what Wieck had said in the review, remarking how the description of the piece was detrimental for Chopin's musical integrity; he did not want the review to be published in Paris. Of course, the ulterior motive behind Wieck writing about the piece so favorably was not to support Chopin, per se, but rather to boost his daughter Clara's performance of the work. Indeed, the *Caecilia* review was accompanied by a short piece written by the editor of the journal, Gottfried Weber, testifying to Clara's skill in performing the work, and Wieck's success in teaching her.

PLEYEL PIANOS

When we think of influences, we often think of teachers, colleagues, contemporaries, but technology must also be counted in the category, for it is the innovations of the tools of creativity that sometimes drive creativity. For Chopin's development to blossom fully, the pianos he used had to respond to the unique demands of his music, and in turn, the idiomatic features of his chosen instruments may have inspired gestures and passages that worked especially well on those keyboards.

When Chopin was eleven years old, French piano manufacturer Sébastien Érard developed and patented the double escapement piano mechanism, a feature that allows a key to be struck multiple times in quick succession because the hammer does not have to return to its full height in between strokes. Works like Liszt's "La Campanella" from his *Grandes études de Paganini* or Chopin's Étude op. 25, no. 2 would not be possible without this technological advancement (also known as "repetition" action). Within a few decades, Erard's contribution—with improvements provided by manufacturer Henri Herz—became the standard action used in the making of grand pianos. Virtuosos, like Liszt especially, solidified the artistic importance of the double escape mechanism.

Another boon was the growing range of the piano. Beethoven's Striecher piano spanned six and a half octaves, which allowed him to write pieces like the Hammerklavier Sonata. The pianos of Chopin's time encompassed a full seven octaves, from the A below the lowest C (still the lowest note on modern pianos) to the G three and a half octaves above middle C (modern pianos go four notes higher to a C). This extensive range was thought of by some to be far too much, but it proved very useful to Chopin and Liszt.

Ignaz Pleyel (1757–1831) founded his piano business in 1807. In addition to having a place for the manufacture of their pianos in Paris, Pleyel et Cie (Pleyel and Company) also had an intimate, 150-seat concert venue called the Salle Pleyel that opened in 1830. Chopin's Parisian debut took place at the Salle Pleyel on February 26, 1832, and naturally, the featured instrument was a Pleyel. Ignaz Pleyel contributed to the development of the piano with the addition of a metal frame to replace the weaker wooden frames of the previous generations. He was also a musician and composer in his own right who had taken composition lessons with Haydn. Son Camille (1788–1855) was a composer as well, who had studied with Dussek. Camille married a prominent pianist of the time: Marie Moke. Kalkbrenner was also associated with the Pleyel family.

The presence of a Pleyel upright in Chopin's studio is proof that the composer respected the brand. The competition between Érard and Pleyel during Chopin's career really depended on what kind of playing felt most comfortable. An Érard was the instrument for Liszt; Érards were larger and louder, and better for public performance (which Chopin often avoided). Chopin preferred the Pleyel—most of the time—as it was perfect in intimate settings like salons, but he played other pianos from time to time. In what sounds like a commercial of sorts for the pianos available to him, Chopin once allegedly said, "When I feel out of sorts, I play on an Érard piano where I easily find a ready-made tone. But when I feel in good form and strong enough to find my own individual sound, then I need a Pleyel piano." It seems the earliest source for this often-quoted tidbit is the book *Musiciens contemporains* (1856) written by music critic and composer Henri Blaze de Bury. Blaze de Bury gives no source for the quote, only mentioning that it was something that "Chopin once said."

Part of the sensitivity of the Pleyel was due to the covering on the hammers inside the instrument. A single layer of hard felt covered in buckskin allowed the striking of the string to produce a tone that emphasized the harmonic overtones of each note. By contrast, the Érard's multiple layers on each hammer emphasized the fundamental of each pitch. The stopping of the sound, or "damping," was likewise different. Piano scholar Robert S. Winter describes the dissimilarity of approaches in the damping:

> Érard's "underdamping" system was spring-loaded to suppress the tone more quickly. Pleyel's overdampers were extremely light and narrow and relied only on gravity, leaving behind a discreet veil of sound even in passages where no sustaining pedal was used.

One can see how Chopin's creativity might have been influenced by this discreet veil of sound, especially in the way he constructed sensitive pieces like the nocturnes. Also, the slightly narrower keys on the Pleyel piano more easily facilitated passages that covered wide ranges, like the right-hand arpeggios of the first étude of op. 10 or the two-hand arpeggios in the last étude of op. 25. It is hard to quantify the kind of influence such features had on Chopin's creativity, but when we view Chopin's relationship with Pleyel, both the brand and the person, we see a level of comfort that could not have helped but encourage the composer's invention and productivity.

9

MALADIES AMONG THE MELODIES

Poe-Chopin, by John B. Tabb (1896):

> O'er each the soul of Beauty flung
> A shadow mingled with the breath
> Of music that the Sirens sung
> Whose utterance is death

From the time he was a young man, Chopin was plagued with health problems. His short life was marked by periods of sickness and periods of relative good health. For many years, historians seemed to agree that he suffered from tuberculosis, although alternative diagnoses have been suggested in this and the last century. This chapter deals with Chopin's health, both physical and mental, and contemporary accounts of his sickness and his final days. There is also an account of a recent attempt to learn more about the circumstances of Chopin's illness by studying his heart, which resides in jar in the wall of a Warsaw church. Chopin's emotional piano sonatas are the musical focus of this chapter.

CONSUMPTION CHIC

In the nineteenth century, there was rich mythology romanticizing death from "consumption." Clark Lawlor, author of a book about consumption in literature, begins his tome with a quote from Edgar Allan Poe's short story "Metzengerstein: A Tale in Imitation of the German." In the opening pages, the unnamed narrator explains the Metzengerstein family history. Specifically, he mentions the death of Lady Mary from consumption: "I would wish all I love to perish of that gentle disease. How glorious! to depart in the hey-day of the young blood—the heart all passion—the imagination all fire—amid the remembrances of happier days—in the fall of the year—and so be buried forever in the gorgeous autumnal leaves!" Seeing death from consumption called "glorious," one can detect the sheen of glamour associated with this disease, as succumbing to it was "as a sign of passion, spirituality and genius," and "a more exalted inner life." The reality of the horror of the ending was a shock for many because of the depiction of consumption as an easy, pain-free death.

Although we think of tuberculosis and consumption as the same thing, "consumption" in the 1800s was a catch-all term for "a range of wasting conditions." The word "tuberculosis," attributed to medical professor Johann Lukas Schönlein, emerged in 1839, a decade before Chopin's death. People in Chopin's circle might have also used the Greek word "phthisis," which was the term for pulmonary tuberculosis. (It comes from the Greek word for wasting.) English physician Richard Morton (1637–1698) had used the word "tubercule," a diminutive form of "tuber," a lump, to name the lesions or swellings found on a consumptive's lungs, heart, or skin. Thought to be a family disease of inheritance, because it often spread through families, the bacteria that causes TB was discovered in 1882 by German physician and bacteriologist Robert Koch. He received the Nobel Prize for this discovery in 1905. Tuberculosis was not, in fact, an inherited disease, but spread by airborne germs. If the disease develops at all (it commonly remains dormant), it can take over quickly—called "galloping"—or it can be chronic. At first, the symptoms are very mild, but get worse with time. Persistent cough is accompanied by weight loss (the wasting seen in "consumption"), a pale complexion, and night sweats.

Chopin was always rather slim and pale, and this made him extremely attractive in the fashion of the time. He was also in great company, as many artists of the time suffered from some consumptive illness or other. Among them were painter Eugène Delacroix, writer Honoré de Balzac, and violin virtuoso, Niccolò Paganini. There were famous characters who suffered tragic consumptive endings, especially Violetta in Verdi's opera *La Traviata* and Mimi in Puccini's *La Bohème*.

Treatment for tuberculosis and other consumptive diseases was limited. Chopin also lived at a time when different methods of diagnosis were emerging. When Chopin took ill on Mallorca in the winter of 1838, he noted what the three doctors who visited did to assess his illness: one doctor examined Chopin's sputum by smelling it; one tapped him on the chest to hear from whence the sputum had come; one listened to him and held him while he expectorated. From these actions the three men had different conclusions that Chopin reported in a letter to Fontana with his typical dark humor: "One said I had died [Chopin used a slang meaning "croaked" or "kicked the bucket"], the second that I am dying, the third that I shall die." He narrowly avoided being bled by leeches on that occasion. On their way to Barcelona, Chopin began coughing up blood. Sand rather dramatically described the voluminous amount of his expectoration as "sinks full."

On this journey back to France via Spain, Chopin was treated by Dr. François Cauvière in Marseilles. Chopin's health steadily improved: his frightful expectorations ceased, he put back on some weight, and slept peacefully. The doctor recommended they stay in Marseilles so as not to encounter bad weather in the north. By May of 1839, he was well enough to undertake a journey to Genoa with Sand and her son, Maurice. The following year saw another decline in Chopin's health. Dr. Paul-Léon-Marie Gaubert, who saw Chopin just after his thirtieth birthday, recommended the following treatments: he was to drink a sugared beverage before leaving bed in the morning, followed by a chest rub with a special pomade; he was to drink an herbal tincture before bed; he was to avoid all excitement (or rather, his companions were supposed to shield him from such); he was to dress warmly; he could drink wine diluted with water. Chopin saw almost three dozen doctors over the course of his life, and not one could offer him anything more than palliative care. One of the treatments in his later years was a tincture of opium-based drops. While it did nothing to alter the course of the disease, it provided some relief from suffering.

Even from childhood, Chopin suffered from health complaints. His childhood doctor, Czesław Sieluzycki, noted a few problems including headaches, tooth decay, gastric issues, shortness of breath, and susceptibility to "rheumatic" diseases. The first reference Chopin makes to his own health exists in a letter he wrote to his friend Jan Białobłocki when he was about fifteen. The culprit: a four-day long headache and swollen glands in the neck. The doctor called this a "catarrhal infection," and Chopin was treated with leeches. His younger sister Emilia suffered from the same thing. After a while, Fryderyk returned to normal. Emilia, however, relapsed and the family decided to take the two ailing children to a spa near the Bohemian border. The "cure" offered there consisted of fresh air, water with a high iron content, and likely sheep or goat's milk. There wasn't a decent instrument for Chopin to play while there, but he ended up playing two concerts anyway, on a substandard piano. Chopin wrote to his friend and explained his days back at home: the doctors recommended lots of walking, six hours of counterpoint lessons with Elsner during the week, lectures on music from Brodzinski and Bentkowski, a nine o'clock bedtime every night, and no socializing. "All teas, evening and balls are off. I drink an emetic water by Malcz's orders, and feed myself only on oatmeal, *quasi* a horse."

When the Chopin family (Fryderyk, Justyna, Ludwika, and Emilia) returned to Warsaw, Fryderyk felt much better, but this didn't last. When Chopin took ill again in early 1827 another trip to the spa was considered, but tragedy precluded the voyage. Emilia died of tuberculosis in April of 1827. She was just fourteen, and her death dealt the family a stunning blow that left them reeling.

Chopin lived until the age of thirty-nine, suffering from a chronic cough for all of his adult life. Accompanying this cough was "abundant expectoration" that necessitated a daily routine to deal with it. George Sand remarked that Chopin coughed with "infinite grace." Her friend, the Countess Marie d'Agoult, stated that Chopin's cough was the only thing about him that was permanent. He was not able to participate in rigorous physical activity, and was quite susceptible to infection. In his final years, he sometimes coughed up blood and purulent sputum (green or yellow mucus filled with pus), and suffered from frequent fevers.

In addition to the physical symptoms, there were thought to be mental consequences as well. Some believed tuberculosis caused schizophrenia, depression, irritability, and an inability to show affection. Chopin displayed some of these traits, but there is no apparent scientific link between these symptoms and the physical illness. Instead, we must look at Chopin's mental health as a separate issue.

FINAL PERFORMANCES AND FINAL ILLNESS

Paris was in the midst of tumultuous times at the beginning of 1848. In February, revolution exploded in France's capital, beginning a wave of revolutions across Europe that spread to dozens of countries. Generally speaking, the working class began to demand more rights, and these demands included some involvement in the political process. Although many of the conflicts in the wave of revolutions ended with little significant change, there were some positive outcomes. The Netherlands, for example, saw the beginning of a parliamentary democracy while Austria ended serfdom. In France, the most significant change with the end of the revolution came the end of the Orleans monarchy and the declaration of the French Second Republic.

It was a few days before this political uprising that Chopin gave what would end up being his very last public concert in France. On Wednesday, February 16, 1848, Chopin performed at the Salle Pleyel. He had been suffering from "a horrible grippe," which had been going around. In a letter, Chopin remarked, "All Paris is sick." Still, he felt well enough to perform a rather lengthy concert. He shared the stage at the beginning with cellist Auguste Franchomme and violinist Jean-Delphin Alard, and the three performed a Mozart piano trio. Following that, Chopin's tour de force included a nocturne, an etude, a barcarolle, a waltz, several preludes and mazurkas, and three-quarters of the Sonata in G minor, assisted by Franchomme.

The performance had been sold out a week earlier, with the king and queen planning to attend. Although Chopin found public concerts quite stressful, he seemed to look forward to the event. Perhaps it seemed to him the culmination of all he had been trying to achieve in his adopted city. It is notable that Chopin was willing to have this concert as he rarely performed in public, finding it taxing on his poor health. He expended his energies on teaching and composing, and the performances he did undertake were usually for intimate gatherings of friends.

Of course, the beautiful Parisian world of aristocrats and royalty was about to experience quite a jolt. The Revolution of 1848 came on the heels of financial crisis, continued unemployment, and impoverishment of the lowest working class. The king, Louis-Philippe, who had risen to power in 1830, was known as Citizen King (*Roi Citoyen*) because he endeavored to dispatch his duties in a more liberal fashion. In a slight but significant change of wording, he wanted to be called the King of the French rather than the King of France. To further show his support of the ideals of the revolution, many of the excesses of previous rulers were eliminated with the king living a more moderate lifestyle. Louis-Philippe's eighteen-year reign saw the growth and support of a financial aristocracy, including bankers and those in charge of natural resources like iron ore, coal, and trees. By 1848, however, Louis-Philippe's attempt to create a middle ground between the monarchy and the revolution had instead created dissatisfaction among many of his subjects. In February of 1848, Louis-Philippe abdicated and fled to England.

Chopin and George Sand, who were by this point estranged, handled the revolution quite differently. Chopin took to bed, bothered as he was by health complaints. Sand, on the other hand, was in many ways the voice of the revolution. She published half a dozen brochures with titles like *A Word to the Middle Class*, and *Letter to the People*. She also used a fictional hero, Blaise Bonnin, whom she had previously invented, in two new essays: *The History of France Dictated by Blaise Bonnin* and *Words of Blaise Bonnin to the Good Citizens*. Blaise Bonnin was a rural day-laborer whose earthy vernacular put the goals of the revolution in plain speech. Bonnin first appeared as the voice for Sand's coverage of a scandal including a young abused girl she called "Fanchette." Risking possible arrest for the scandalous story, Sand backed up her story with factual sources.

Although her name came up as a possible candidate for the National Assembly, Sand averred that women should only enter politics after sweeping reforms in society had taken place. Political equality could not be possible without first allowing women the same educational opportunities as men and a similar societal standing. One might argue that these things might come faster with women in positions of power in a government, but Sand appeared to see things differently. As authors Richard Keeble and Sharon Wheeler put it, "The class struggle came before the women's struggle." By June, the combined faction of middle and working classes that had revolted had split. The *petit bourgeoisie* abandoned the working class, and the revolution soon fell apart. George Sand, disappointed by the events, used her public influence to beg for clemency for many of the revolutionaries, but soon went back to writing literature.

Chopin, having left George Sand's circle of friends, was not politically involved. He was more concerned with maintaining his status quo: teaching, composing, socializing. Sand's daughter, Solange, with whom he was still close, had recently given birth to her second child. Chopin wrote to her, "the birth of your daughter gave me greater joy than the birth of the Republic." During a chance meeting with Sand soon after, Chopin was the person who told Sand of her new grandchild. Unfortunately, the child was not to survive a week.

Although he seemed fairly indifferent to the revolution in France, he was hopeful about revolutionary events happening in Poland. He was sufficiently heartened to write about the possibilities to his friend Julian Fontana. Not much came of the wave of revolution in Poland, however, and Chopin began to cast his thoughts to not returning, nor to even staying in Paris. Many aristocratic families had left the city, and Chopin saw his supply of wealthy students dry up. He had written nothing new for his publishers, and despite his fragile health, made plans to visit England and Scotland.

Jane Wilhelmina Stirling, a Scottish woman who had been Chopin's student, made all of the plans for Chopin's travels. He had three pianos at his disposal in the apartment he was renting, but barely had time to use them. He played private performances, met up with the important members of London high society, attended the opera at Covent Garden, and saw some old friends who were in England coincidentally. He played for Queen Victoria and many other dignitaries in May. He was offered the opportunity to play a piano concerto with the London Philharmonic Society Orchestra, but turned it down. Instead, he attempted to make money with private performances, but found it quite difficult, as many members of the aristocracy were not willing to pay his fee.

His health deteriorated, and Chopin was often exhausted by the constant activity. In summer, he reported to his friend Grzymała, "My health varies from hour to hour; but often in the mornings it seems as if I must cough my life out." And his complaints were not only physical. He spoke in letters about avoiding solitude because it bred sad thoughts. George Sand, though not in his life, was still in his head. He sometimes asked his friends for information about her. Being away for months in England and Scotland, under the watchful eyes of Stirling and her sister, Katherine Erskine, was an escape from that Parisian world so associated with Sand. But it came at a steep price; he was physically exhausted, and was expected to make appearances, meet people, and sightsee. He found the scenery beautiful and the people hospitable, but his body was tired. Upon his return to London, he spent nearly three weeks in bed with a bad cold.

He was well enough to attend and perform at a charity concert at the Guildhall organized by Lord Stuart. Chopin played two Études from the op. 25 collection and a few other pieces, but he was fatigued, and the audience was not of a mind to sit quietly and listen to sensitive piano music while lively dancing was available in the other rooms. His last public appearance as a pianist was described by historian Francis Hueffer as "a well-intentioned mistake." He arrived back in Paris in late November of 1848. The February Revolution had ultimately failed, and the December election brought in a new president, Prince Charles Louis-Napoleon Bonaparte.

Chopin spent his final months sketching out some works: a mazurka, a nocturne, a waltz. He continued to correspond with Solange, who had mended fences with George Sand. Both Chopin and Sand were anxious for word about each other, but never corresponded directly. Singer and friend to both parties, Pauline Viardot was in contact with each of them. Chopin seemed to understand how little time he had left, and so he began to make his final requests. He reached out to his sister Ludwika to visit. "No doctors can help me as much as you," he said in a letter to her.

Biographer Tad Szulc marks June 22, 1849, as the beginning of the end for Chopin. Unable to teach or compose, he was running out of money, and his kind mother sent some to funds to run his house. On the night of the twenty-second, Chopin appears to have suffered multiple hemorrhages, which caused him to cough up blood. Eventually, and through the intervention of friends, Dr. Cruveilhier was summoned to Chopin's apartment on rue Challiot. By July, Cruveilhier had prescribed a homeopathic medicine with lichen, thought to treat consumption. By the end of August, Cruveilhier asked two of his colleagues for their opinions about Chopin's condition and what should be done. They all agreed that travel was out, but that Chopin needed to be warmer in general. So the composer moved apartments to one in central Paris on Place Vendôme.

George Sand reached out to Chopin's sister to find out more about her ex-lover, but heard nothing back. Even perhaps sensing that time was short, there was to be no reconciliation. Chopin did, however, wish to see Tytus Wojciechowski, his childhood friend. Despite the desperation of Chopin's tone, the two did not get a chance to see each other again. Ludwika stayed, even after her family returned to Warsaw. Friend Delfina Potocka heard the news of Chopin's suffering and rushed to his side. He asked her to sing, and so the piano was brought into Chopin's sick room, and Potocka sang as her friend struggled for breath.

Chopin was desperately afraid of being buried alive, so he wrote—in shaky hand—that he wished to be "opened" so that his death could be confirmed. At the moment of Chopin's death, there were half a dozen people present, including his sister Ludwika, Solange Sand, and Adolf Gutmann. Among Chopin's final wishes, besides an autopsy, were that his unfinished manuscripts be burned, his Piano Method bestowed upon Charles-Valentin Alkan, and that the music at his funeral be Mozart's *Requiem*. After his death, the doctor performed the autopsy, removing Chopin's heart and placing it into a jar of alcohol.

RETROSPECTIVE DIAGNOSIS

As medical science identifies and defines illnesses and conditions, there sometimes comes research claiming that a historical figure suffered from this or that, based on contemporary evidence. Or there is a desire to learn the "truth" of someone's medical history. In the nearly two centuries since Beethoven's death, for example, scientists have written about the possible causes of Beethoven's deafness including proliferative meningitis, otitis media, syphilis, labyrinthitis, and Paget's disease of bone. In studying contemporary accounts of sickness—letters, journal entries, autopsy reports, doctors' notes—modern physicians and scientists may make retrospective diagnoses. In rare cases, there are physical specimens to examine, for example, a lock of Beethoven's hair, a fragment of bone, or even a preserved organ. In some cases, exhumation may be granted by surviving family. Retrospective diagnoses are notoriously difficult to prove with any degree of certainty, even with physical evidence, although in most cases none exists. But there is an undeniable desire among many music historians to understand—as much as it is possible—the context of a composer's life and death, the day-to-day canvas upon which timeless art was created.

Before we used the term "retrospective diagnosis," there existed a literary genre known as pathography, in which biographical sketches were made with particular focus on illness. These are useful insofar as they illuminate the context of creation—especially over long periods of illness. That context consists of a combination of a number of factors. Take social interactions, for example. We may see if illness negatively affected the artist's ability to perform or to make social connections. Depending on how the public viewed the particular disease (or even the symptoms), we might see an impact on an artist's acceptance. In Paris, during Chopin's heyday, tuberculosis was not understood as a virulently transmissible disease, otherwise Chopin might not have had a steady stream of wealthy students coming to interact with him in close quarters. In Mallorca, in contrast, worry over contagion caused social rejection (unhelped by Sand's scandalous reputation on that Catholic island) and eviction from their rooms. After word went around that Chopin's medical crisis was a result of tuberculosis, Señor Gomez, the landlord of the property, demanded their immediate departure and financial restitution for the disinfection of their villa and the destruction (through fire) of the infected bedding and furniture. Chopin had no such issues in France or England, renting apartments without question and holding intimate salons with members of the wealthy class.

It makes less sense to worry about "accurately" diagnosing an illness that had no bearing on a composer's career overall, nor does it really matter in the grand scheme of things. Furthermore, the change in retrospective diagnoses often reflects current trends in medical discovery. Recent years have seen many historical figures—Albert Einstein, Nikola Tesla, Andy Warhol, Emily Dickinson—retrospectively placed on the autism spectrum by various researchers. And diagnosis of a collection of symptoms is of less importance than the symptoms themselves, especially as described in first-person accounts. But there is the unstoppable curiosity that attaches to artists. Knowing everything possible to be known is the prerogative of the biographer and the fan alike. Speculation may infect the proceedings, so to speak. What follows is simply a report on what has been said, and not an endorsement of any particular diagnosis.

For many years, it was regarded as fact that the "consumption" suffered by Chopin was caused by tuberculosis. But there has been speculation for many decades as to the veracity of this claim. The main source of evidence has been contemporary accounts—George Sand's description of her lover's cough, testimony of students who witnessed Chopin's weak constitution on lesson days, accounts of the friends who were there for the final weeks, Chopin's letters to friends—but what physical evidence could be used to confirm or deny the diagnosis of tuberculosis?

After Chopin's death on October 17, 1849, his doctor, Jean Cruveilhier—Paris's foremost authority on TB—performed the autopsy that Chopin had desperately requested the day before his death. During the procedure, Dr. Cruveilhier removed Chopin's heart and placed it in a jar of alcohol. This alcohol, probably cognac, preserved the heart for the ensuing century and a half. Many visitors to Paris have seen the grave of Chopin at the Père Lachaise Cemetery, but it contains the body of the composer without its heart. Chopin's heart was returned to Poland. The story goes that the heart had to be smuggled into the country, past the Russian border guards. This feat was likely performed by Chopin's sister Ludwika, who might have hidden the jar underneath her skirt. When the heart arrived, the jar was sealed into a pillar at the Holy Cross Church in Warsaw. There it stayed ostensibly until April 2014, when a team of thirteen people removed it from the pillar. Among this team were two scientists, including forensic scientist Tadeusz Dobosz. The archbishop of Warsaw was also present. They reportedly performed this secret task in the middle of the night.

The heart was not cut open nor was any tissue removed. It was not even removed from the jar. The team did take more than a thousand photographs of Chopin's heart, and reported upon visual inspection that the organ had held up well. It was larger than an average heart, suggesting respiratory problems, as one might expect. The team was able to see nodules of tissue they assumed were from tuberculosis. Sebastian Lucas, a doctor who was not among the viewers in Poland, suggested that a visual scan of the tissue could not suggest a conclusive diagnosis. Pericarditis, an inflammation around the heart consistent with TB, could show as nodules, like the ones seen on Chopin's heart. But Lucas also suggested that these nodules could be evidence of cancer or a fungal infection. For one to be sure, further invasive tests must

be done. But no one is quite ready for that to happen. Rose Cholmon-
deley, head of the Chopin Society, used the word "desecration" to describe that process, as if the status of Chopin had changed in death from
regular person to saint.

There is also a possibility that since Chopin's death in 1849, a
circumstance might have arisen in which the heart was removed and
replaced with another one. There is a story that says a German soldier
removed the heart for safe keeping during the Second World War. The
commander of German forces, General Erich von dem Bach-Zelewski,
was supposedly one of the protectors of the heart in this story. The
general was in charge of quashing the Warsaw Uprising of 1944. Ironic
then that he would put effort into protecting the relic. But again, this is
just a story, without much evidence behind it. Although this could have
happened, Dobosz, who was actually at the church during the 2014
secret operation, found that for him all doubts were dispelled. He noted
the type of jar and the type of thread used to sew up the heart after it
had been examined were "of the era." Once the secret procedure was
complete, the heart was returned to the pillar, and all parties agreed
that it should not again be disturbed for another half century.

Although Chopin's death certificate notes the cause of death as TB,
according to Dr. Cruveilhier, apparently there seemed to be some un-
certainty about that. The doctor made some notes, now lost, that may
have made reference to some question about the final diagnosis. Jane
Stirling, in a letter to Franz Liszt, said that the doctor said something to
the effect of the heart being more affected than the lungs, a condition
he had not seen before. This has opened the door for speculation. In
1987, J. G. O'Shea suggested that Chopin suffered from cystic fibrosis,
a disease that was defined in 1938 by Dorothy Hansine Andersen. It is a
hereditary disease that affects and inhibits the functioning of certain
and glands and organs. The lungs are usually affected, as are the pan-
creas and gastrointestinal tract. The abnormal production of mucus is a
central issue, as is a predisposition to respiratory infections that must be
treated with antibiotics. Recurrent pneumonia is a particular worry for
many patients. The inhibition of pancreatic function causes intolerance
of fatty foods, which cannot be digested. In men, the proliferation of
mucus in the vas deferens usually causes infertility.

Certain conditions of Chopin's life—lack of facial hair, his chronic
diarrhea (and abhorrence of fatty foods), and joint pain—support this

theory. Also, George Sand seemingly never contracted this disease despite their sometimes very close quarters. Chopin fathered no children, although it is uncertain how sexually active he was. Of course if he did have cystic fibrosis, it would likely have been an atypical cystic fibrosis, which is less severe. Most sufferers of all forms of this disease—even in the mid-twentieth century—did not live past the age of twenty. And still now with the most advanced medical breakthroughs, current sufferers have a life expectancy of about thirty-eight years.

In 1994, J. A. Kuzemko argued, on the basis of Chopin's correspondence, that Chopin suffered not from tuberculosis or cystic fibrosis but instead an antitrypsin deficiency, a condition in which the alpha-antitrypsin level in the blood is too low. There are genetic variants for this disease, some indicate liver disease, while others indicate respiratory issues. Some variants see both lungs and liver affected by the disease. Sufferers of antitrypsin deficiency may experience labored breathing, recurrent respiratory infection, or asthma. In other variants, patients may have liver problems including impaired function all the way to cirrhosis and liver failure. If Chopin's sister Emilia had also suffered from antitrypsin deficiency, it would be a possible explanation for her hematemesis (vomiting of blood). Cirrhosis, an extreme condition of antitrypsin deficiency, could cause portal hypertension. The scar tissue from cirrhosis causes a blockage of blood to the liver. Pressure builds up the portal vein, forcing the blood into other, smaller veins. Often the blood travels to the veins in the lower esophagus (the tube connecting the mouth and stomach), which are too thin to handle the extra flow. When they rupture, as they often do, the patient will likely vomit blood. A diagnosis of antitrypsin deficiency with both liver and lungs involved would explain Chopin's respiratory problems and recurrent infections, his gastrointestinal issues, and his inability to gain a significant amount of weight.

Since 1899 there have been additional medical interpretations of Chopin's illness. Anemia was added as an alternative to the TB diagnosis in 1935; allergy was floated as a possible cause in 1961; mitral stenosis was suggested in 1964. Since O'Shea's discussion of cystic fibrosis in 1987, there have been more supporters of either cystic fibrosis and antitrypsin deficiency, but tuberculosis remains the top diagnosis. Statistically, tuberculosis remains the most likely candidate; even today, nearly 30 percent of the world's population asymptomatically carry this

disease or actively suffer from it. Axel Karenberg has meticulously catalogued all the diagnoses offered to date of Chopin's condition, noting
that even a definitive diagnosis of something besides TB would leave
Chopin's musical legacy entirely unchanged.

INSIDE CHOPIN'S HEAD

Ancient medical beliefs of the Greek and Roman civilization held that
there were four humors—bodily liquids—at balance in the body, a state
called *eucrasia*. These four humors were black bile (*melaina chole*),
yellow bile (*chole*), phlegm (*phlegma*), and blood (*haima*). If there occurred some imbalance of these humors, or *dyscrasia*, disease would
follow. A proliferation of black bile, for example, would cause "melancholia." If one suffered from melancholia, symptoms could be similar to
what we describe now as depression and anxiety. Chopin often suffered
from bouts of what his contemporaries likely referred to as "melancholy" (*mélancolie* in French).

Chopin's chronic physical suffering likely had a profound effect on
his mental state. We see particularly difficult issues when his body was
in crisis. One Chopin scholar described the mercurial temperament the
composer experienced: "Chopin's usual courtesy, even playfulness,
could give way on days of illness or irritability to fits of anger, as violent
as they were brief." During the disastrous winter in Mallorca, Chopin
wrote to friend Wojciech Grzymała, "The world is as black as my heart."
After their departure, George Sand remarked to the Contessa Marliani,
"Another month and Chopin would have died of melancholy in Spain."

There is more to the story than that, of course. Even in relatively
stable physical health, Chopin was sometimes overcome by depressive
moods. In the autumn of 1830, Chopin and his friend Tytus Wojciechowski traveled through Dresden and Prague with a final destination
of Vienna. It is at this point that we first begin to see turmoil in Chopin's inner life: "I find everything here so sad, gloomy, and melancholic," he wrote in a letter to Jan Matuszyński. He further characterized his
tearless, but sad mood as a "dry melancholy." This letter is dated the
day after Christmas of 1830. He was away from his family during the
holiday, which might explain some of his gloom. The trip to Vienna was
ultimately not any kind of professional breakthrough either. A few days

after Christmas, he spoke to Matuszyński of his self-doubt by saying, "I am worthless to my fellow men." Even in this state of turmoil, Chopin continued to create. "I pour my despair out over the piano," was how he put it.

Writing music was a way for him to take his sadness and melancholy and put them to use. Axel Karenberg sums it up this way: "Chopin's compositional work after 1830 was a kind of self-therapy designed to transpose and transform constant, recurring depression into musical creations." Karenberg also looks at speculation concerning Chopin's mental state. Among the diagnoses on this front are schizoid personality, depressive personality, pseudo-schizophrenia, impotence, and asexuality. Karenberg notes, "the less that is known, the greater room for speculation."

In 2011, Spanish researchers attempted to find a medical explanation for the hallucinations that Chopin sometimes experienced. Sand recalled this in her memoirs: "Though he bore [physical] pain with passable courage, he could not overcome his anxiety-ridden fancies. For him the cloister [in Mallorca] was full of phantoms and terrors even when he was well." Chopin described these hallucinations himself and of course we have the testimony of his contemporaries. The authors of this study, Manuel Vázquez Caruncho and Francisco Brañas Fernández, say that temporal lobe epilepsy was likely the cause of Chopin's hallucinations. They ruled out various other causes like migraine auras, eye disorders, and opium-induced hallucinations from the opium drops (laudanum) he took to stop his cough. One of the experiences described by Chopin in which he saw such a thing was a year before his death in 1848. He was playing a rare concert in public, about to begin a piece (the Funeral March discussed below), when he was beset by visions: "suddenly, I saw emerging from the half-open case of my piano those cursed creatures that had appeared to me on a lugubrious night at the Carthusian monastery." Temporal lobe epilepsy may cause what are known as partial seizures. A person with seizures of this type may not lose consciousness and may just experience auditory, visual, gustatory, or olfactory hallucinations. So the person may smell something, taste something, see, or hear something abnormal.

In addition to melancholy, Chopin sometimes suffered from bouts of anger. Biographer Tad Szulc describes "typically manic-depressive mood swings. . . . During attacks of rage, he smashed chairs, broke

pencils, and heaped invective upon hapless piano students or visitors."
In her memoirs, George Sand said, "Chopin in a rage was fearsome, and
since with me he always restrained himself, he seemed likely to burst
and die." In 1996, Dr. Kay Redfield Jamison (Johns Hopkins University
School of Medicine) published a book, *Touched With Fire: Manic-Depressive Illness and the Artistic Temperament*. Although she does not
diagnose Chopin specifically, based on her description of symptoms,
Chopin might very well be a candidate. Chopin sometimes suffered
emotional outbursts, he had a preoccupation with death, could be indecisive and easily distracted. These, of course, are rather broad behaviors
that could be indicative of many conditions. And it should be noted that
people who suffer from chronic physical disease often have emotional
symptoms as well. When the body suffers so much, the mind cannot be
unaffected.

PIANO SONATAS

Chopin "poured out" his despair into piano pieces. He composed three
piano sonatas over the course of his career. The first dates from Chopin's teenage years and is rarely performed in public. It was dedicated
to Józef Elsner, who was Chopin's teacher at the time, and it adheres in
some ways to the traditional forms, but it has a couple of surprises. It is
a carefree and jaunty piece, reflecting the young Chopin, so full of hope
and potential. There are four movements, a majestic Allegro, a minuet,
a Larghetto third movement, and a Presto finale. The style is somewhat
derivative of the models he had at the time, notably that of Hummel.
The trio of the second movement minuet is particularly charming and
reminiscent of this transitional style from Classicism to Romanticism.
One of the surprising elements of this sonata is a third movement in 5/4
time, a very unusual choice. The finale is likely the most memorable
part of the sonata, with a vivacious opening theme, and an insistent
tempo that drives the movement forward. Hints of the mature Chopin
are here in the perpetual motion and the lush sonorities, but the best
was still to come.

The other two piano sonatas date from later years, one written in
1839 and one in 1844. Chopin's Piano Sonata No. 3 in B minor was
composed when Chopin was thirty-four years old, and it was in these

years that he was perhaps beginning to truly understand the fragility of his health. Chopin was not able to give adequate time to composition while teaching and maintaining his status in Parisian society, so he composed mostly during summers at George Sand's estate in Nohant. The Piano Sonata in B minor, one of the works from Nohant, is a large-scale work in four movements. Although Chopin's composition was intimately tied to his playing, this was one work not premiered by Chopin, nor did he ever play it in a public performance. It has an emotional and noble opening movement, a light Molto Vivace second movement, a graceful Largo, and an astounding virtuosic finale. All of the hallmarks of Chopin's style are here: tumultuous and talented playing, shifting moods, lyrical melodies, and an almost unbearable sense of longing. It is a true masterpiece and represents the culmination of a lifetime (albeit short) of piano playing.

The Piano Sonata No. 2 in B-flat minor, op. 35 acts as the finale of this discussion, as it is the most famous of the three sonatas of Chopin. It is known by many as "The Funeral March," named for the remarkable third movement. He completed the work in 1839. There is no shortage of drama in this sonata, especially in the first and last movements. Chopin uses his considerable gifts for innovative harmony here, and the work consistently impresses, especially in the virtuosic conclusion. Contemporary critics didn't know quite what to make of the sonata at first, but this is not surprising, considering that this work seems to mark the transition into Chopin's mature style. Schumann's review of the work from 1841 admonished that Chopin had included "obstacles on almost every page," making the work too difficult for the avid pianist to play. Schumann even suggested that Chopin's progressions and notations were willfully designed to be indecipherable.

The third movement, the Funeral March, has taken on something of a life of its own as a stand-alone piece. It was orchestrated by Henry Wood (of the London Proms concerts) on two separate occasions around the turn of the twentieth century. Sir Edward Elgar (1857–1934) provided an orchestration in 1833. Conductor Leopold Stokowski orchestrated the work as well. Arrangements for this piece have been played at the funerals of important dignitaries, including John F. Kennedy. The piece was, of course, played for Chopin himself when he was buried at Père Lachaise Cemetery.

A brief finale ends the sonata. Although quite short in duration, it remains something of an enigma in its design. Chopin described this movement to his friend Fontana as unison "gossip" for the left and right hand. Chopin biographer Siepmann describes it this way:

> These three pages, which Chopin so casually dismisses as gossip, may well constitute the most enigmatic movement in the entire history of the sonata idea. As a self-contained prelude, less than ninety seconds long, it would be astonishing enough; as the conclusion of a major virtuoso work of more than twenty minutes duration, it simply takes the breath away. Its weirdness is timeless. Its restlessness eternal. If this is gossip, it is the gossiping of demons.

Artur Rubinstein characterized this section as the "wind howling around the gravestones." Chopin was always cagey about sharing his thoughts about the meanings of his pieces (assuming there were intended meanings), and the finale of Sonata No. 2 in B-flat minor remains one of the most often discussed movements in his work. The mystery around what idea lurks at its heart remains; however, one thing is certain. For Chopin, there was something to be said or expressed *after* the funeral march, whether it be the wind howling, demons gossiping, or simply a final virtuosic display. In this case, the music alone has the last word.

10

MODERN CHOPIN

THE ENDURING CULTURAL LEGACY

The life of Chopin ended in 1849, but his life and work gave us a legacy that endures today. Works like Chopin's études, preludes, and waltzes are taught to young promising pianists, ensuring that Chopin's art lives on, continually programmed on concerts and appreciated in classrooms. But Chopin's music has also taken on another life as part of popular culture. It is part of film, television, and video game soundtracks; it is a cultural object rich in associations—Romanticism, refinement, expressive emotion. Chopin himself has been portrayed on screen in multiple films, sometimes as the supporting player in another story (as in the Liszt biopic, *Song Without End*), but at least three times in a starring role. In 2007, Namco Bandai Games published *Eternal Sonata*, a role-playing video game that envisions the dreams of Chopin in the final hours before his death. An even more recent app game has Chopin facing off against modern-day musicians. This chapter discusses Chopin's presence in popular culture as a character in films and video games, and also delves into the use of Chopin's music as accompaniment to various media.

CHAPTER 10

CHOPIN IN ANIMATION

Any child who grew up in the latter half of the twentieth century likely encountered classical music as part of an animated short film. Whether it was the Wagner pastiche in *What's Opera Doc?* or Rossini's *Barber of Seville* in *The Rabbit of Seville*, cartoons—particularly Looney Tunes—familiarized many classical pieces to the viewing audience. The cartoon scores of Carl Stalling (1891–1972), for example, were often peppered with classical pieces.

The music of Fryderyk Chopin appears in a number of the Looney Tunes short films. Daniel Goldmark, specialist on the use of classical music in animation, states, "Chopin is represented in cartoons almost entirely by the opening four-note motif of his *Funeral March*." But there are quite a few other specific examples. In *Hyde and Hare*, a 1955 cartoon short with music by Carl Stalling featuring Bugs Bunny, Bugs finds a score on a piano and gets ready to play. He reads: "Minute Waltz, by Chopin." He pronounces "minute" as in small, and says "Choppin" rather than "Chopin." There is also a reference to popular pianist Liberace as Bugs turns to the audience and says, "I wish my brother George was here." (Liberace was influenced by the Chopin biopic *A Song to Remember*, discussed below.) An orchestration of Chopin's "Raindrop" Prelude appears in Stalling's score to *Water, Water Everyhare*. The music appropriately accompanies flowing water as it fills up Bugs's home.

Chopin's (and other classical composers') presence in these cartoons is due in no small measure to Carl Stalling, whose unique personal history helped shape the first classical music experiences of several generations. Stalling had begun his career—at the tender age of twelve—as a cinema organist in his hometown of Lexington, Missouri. Like many organists for silent films and cartoons, his repertoire consisted of classical tunes along with music improvised to the actions on screen. He was very good at this work, and by the time he was in his twenties, he had his own orchestra and an organist job in Kansas City.

He met another creative young man named Walt Disney, who saw plenty of potential in Carl Stalling. The two collaborated on a few shorts, and their work together and discussions about music and animation eventually encouraged Disney to develop *Silly Symphonies. Silly Symphonies* cartoons, the first of which saw its debut in 1929, were something of a workshop in which Disney's artists could experiment with music and animation. The results of their work include seventy-five stand-alone short films, and their influence on contemporary and subsequent projects like *Snow White and the Seven Dwarfs* (1937), though less quantifiable, is unmistakable. Disney's ambitious "concert" feature, *Fantasia* (1940), would not have been possible without these experiments.

One of the main issues involved in the *Silly Symphonies* was how to synchronize music to picture. Stalling composed the music to twenty-one short films for Disney, including the very first *Silly Symphony*, *The Skeleton Dance*. The piece of music Stalling created was given to the animators after it was complete, requiring them to focus their animation to keep in time with the storyboards. Animator and composer Wilfred Jackson had previously developed a system called "bar sheets" that allowed the cartoon's visual storyboard to include a musical storyboard that would mark the places where music would appear and match musical cues with particular actions. This allowed for greater synchronicity between music and picture. There's actually a term for music that matches perfectly to an on-screen action—think a descending scale for someone walking down a set of stairs, for example; it's called "mickey-mousing." Often used pejoratively when it occurs in dramatic live-action, it was essential for these animated shorts and features, and Stalling was a master at it.

After leaving Disney, Stalling was hired by producer Leon Schlesinger as a full-time cartoon composer for Warner Bros. Stalling worked for the studio for twenty-two years, producing roughly a complete score a week, especially for Looney Tunes. Stalling's compositional style for these cartoons was heavily influenced by his experience as a cinema organist. They include many classical music references, popular tunes, and newly written scores. Stalling's scores turned on a dime, matching the sometimes absurd actions on screen, and requiring split-second timing to make it all work. Stalling was known for making musical puns and inside jokes, sometimes using established clichés from the 1930s and sometimes creating his own. The musical language of these cartoons was established and reinforced over decades of production. The success of Stalling's musical scores would not have been possible without the stellar talents of the studio musicians who played in the Warner Bros. Orchestra.

But Carl Stalling and Looney Tunes weren't the only ones using classical music and the music of Chopin in their short films. Disney's *Silly Symphonies* and Warner Bros.' Looney Tunes inspired Universal, who had their own version with Musical Miniatures, which ran from 1946 to 1948. One of them presented *Musical Moments from Chopin*, featuring Andy Panda and Woody Woodpecker. The piano duo of Saidenberg and Rebner provided performances of a number of pieces by Chopin, including Polonaise in A-flat major, the Fantasie-Impromptu in C-sharp minor, and the Mazurka in B-flat major. The premise is rather simple: piano soloist Andy Panda gives a recital in a barn. Woody Woodpecker comes out on stage to polish the piano, but ends up joining in the performance. They begin their collaboration on the same piano, but eventually, Woody moves to his own piano while they duet. In the meantime, cutaways to the audience, which is made up of various animals, provide comic relief. A couple of these funny scenes are based on the premise that people are trying to be quiet; in one, a character tries to keep another from sneezing, while in another, a whole group of audience members pounce on dog trying to open candy that is wrapped in crinkly paper.

Romantic piano music was definitely part of the zeitgeist of that time. *Musical Moments from Chopin*, made a year after *A Song to Remember*, was nominated for an Academy Award. The cartoon short it lost the award to was Tom and Jerry's *A Cat Concerto*, a short film featuring Franz Liszt's Hungarian Rhapsody No. 2. That same year a Warner Bros. cartoon used the same piece by Liszt (and a similar premise) in its short, *Rhapsody Rabbit*.

Tom and Jerry presented their own concert of Chopin's music in their 1964 short *Snowbody Loves Me* (the German title is *Spiele mit dem Feuer*, or *Play with Fire*). The short was directed by Chuck Jones and Maurice Noble and features music by Eugene Poddany. (That same year Poddany folded the music of Rossini into the narrative and score of another Tom and Jerry short, *The Cat Above and the Mouse Below*.) The score for *Snowbody Loves Me* is a collection of orchestrated fragments from various piano pieces from Chopin, including études, waltzes, and the Fantasie-Impromptu. Tom and Jerry are in the Swiss Alps. Tom is warm inside of what looks like a home/cheese shop. Jerry, who is freezing outside, finds a way in, and infiltrates a giant wheel of Emmentaler cheese. The Chopin excerpts are fully integrated into the orchestral score, sometimes transitioning seamlessly from one into another, sometimes giving way to a newly written section of music. There's no overt narrative reason why Chopin's music was used in this particular cartoon, unlike the Musical Miniature that featured Chopin's music as concert repertoire. Here, Chopin's music simply provides suitable incidental music for the actions on screen.

CHOPIN ON FILM, PART 1: THE PATRIOT

During World War II, filmmakers endeavored to find narratives designed to uplift a public that had given their best men and many of their resources to the war effort. Some of these films were overtly military in nature, while others were quietly political. At first glance, one might not assume that a biopic about Fryderyk Chopin could be used for political propaganda, but that is indeed part of the thrust of 1944's *A Song to Remember*. This highly fictionalized account of the life and career of Chopin (Cornel Wilde)—with great emphasis on his love affair with George Sand (Merle Oberon)—is a portrait of an artist devoted to freedom and his homeland until a temptress lures him into selfish pursuits and away from his true calling.

The circle of people around Chopin in director Charles Vidor's portrait is quite small indeed. There is teacher Józef Elsner (Paul Muni), who has a dual role in Chopin's life: that of teacher and promoter, and that of moral conscience. It is Elsner who encourages young Fryderyk's involvement in politics, and he who finds ways to hide this involvement from his protégé's family. It is also Elsner who suggests Chopin leave Poland for bigger and better opportunities in Paris. It is this relationship that is the most strained by the presence of George Sand. At first, it is only with Sand's influence and intervention that Chopin finds public success in Paris, but then her desire to keep him locked away from the world causes the crisis. This small circle also includes Franz Liszt (Stephen Bekassy), who uses his own renown to help Chopin. Rounding out the cast are George Coulouris as Pleyel, Howard Freeman as Kalkbrenner, and Nina Foch as Constantia, who is likely Konstancja Gładkowska, Chopin's early love interest.

The opening scene, which takes place when Chopin is a child, gives us two pieces of information: (1) Chopin is a child prodigy, and (2) this

eleven-year-old child is already showing the makings of a political revolutionary. The film creates a situation where the teenaged Chopin, making his important debut, refuses to play for Russian dignitaries, calling
them "tsarist butchers" when they enter the party. In the film, he leaves
under cover of the night to avoid arrest, and later finds out that two of
his friends were beaten to death for aiding in his escape. The real
Chopin was never this overtly political, certainly not this vociferously.
Prominent in the score is an orchestrated version of Chopin's "Revolutionary" Étude. Also heard is Chopin's "Heroic" Polonaise.

The film sets up a crisis of the desires of the individual over the
greater good. In wartime, this conflict is thrown into sharper relief. The
situation in Poland worsens, and Elsner goes to visit Chopin, whom he
has not seen in a long time. Sand defends the decision to keep Chopin
away from the public eye, citing his frail health and his genius, which
needs to be nurtured. Elsner argues, but eventually leaves. To Chopin,
he gives a small bag of earth from Poland, brought by one of the composer's old friends. Reminded of his responsibility to his homeland,
Chopin embarks on a European tour to raise money for the war effort.
Sand protests, saying the effort of such a tour would amount to suicide,
but Chopin cannot be dissuaded. A montage of his performances follows, and we see the composer get weaker and more frail with each
appearance. On his deathbed, he asks for Sand, but she does not come.
He dies without seeing her again.

There were four musical forces at work in A Song to Remember.
There is Chopin himself, whose music forms the heart of many scenes,
as Cornel Wilde's Chopin plays pieces for various audiences. There is
José Iturbi who did all of the piano playing for the film (Ervin
Nyiregyházi's hands appear on camera), and who also orchestrated part
of Chopin's B minor Sonata. There is also Miklós Rósza, who is listed as
music adapter, and Morris Stoloff, who was the music director of Columbia Pictures at the time.

The film was nominated for a few Academy Awards including Best
Actor (Cornel Wilde), Editing, Cinematography, Best Writing (Original
Story), and Best Music (Score of a Dramatic or Comedy Picture). For
this latter category, the two nominees were Miklós Rósza and Morris
Stoloff. Stoloff began his career as a violinist, studying with Leopold
Auer. After a stint with the Los Angeles Philharmonic, he joined the
Paramount Studios Orchestra, and was concertmaster for that ensem-

ble. From there Stoloff became musical director for Columbia Pictures from 1936 to 1962. It was a new position, and Stoloff proved himself adept at providing musical support for all the films produced by a very busy studio. He might have been involved in the actual composition of scores, or involved in the organization of recording a score, finding musicians, setting up the actual recording sessions, and the like. For this work, he sometimes received a co-credit as a composer. He was nominated by the Academy of Motion Pictures eighteen times for Musical Direction. He won three times: for *Cover Girl* (1944), *The Jolson Story* (1946), and *Song Without End* (1960). *Song Without End* is about Franz Liszt, also directed by Charles Vidor.

The other nominee was Miklós Rósza, a Hungarian-born, German-trained composer who wrote almost a hundred film scores. His mother, Rósza's first music teacher, had studied piano with teachers who had studied with Franz Liszt. Like the Chopin of *A Song to Remember*, Rósza was performing and writing music at a young age, and was thoroughly interested in the folk music of Hungary. He left Budapest to study in Germany at the Leipzig Conservatory, after a brief period as a chemistry student. He composed art music, moving to Paris, and then London before finding his way to the United States and finally Hollywood. At first, writing film scores was just a way to support his efforts as a concert composer, but Rósza took to it easily. He composed film scores steadily from 1937 to 1982. He was nominated for sixteen Academy Awards and walked away with three. (One of those Oscar statues was for *Spellbound*, a score that he composed in the same year as *A Song to Remember*, and *The Lost Weekend*. He is to date the only composer who won the category and had two other nominated films. *Spellbound* was notable because Rósza used the theremin, a unique electronic instrument with an eerie sound.)

The fourth musical force at work in *A Song to Remember* was pianist José Iturbi. An article in the *New York Times* from January 26, 1945, states: "José Iturbi, the unseen and unbilled double for Chopin (Cornel Wilde) at the piano, is the real star of the picture, for it is the score which sings most brilliantly." The reason why he could not be billed was because he was under contract to MGM and could only work for other studios if he remained uncredited. He received a payment of $35,000 for his work. Iturbi further profited when his record company, Victor Red Seal Records, decided to put out an album in 1945, cashing in on the success of *A Song to Remember*. It was called *Music to Remember, from the Life of Chopin*. In August of that year, Iturbi recorded a single of Chopin's Polonaise in A-flat. It sold over a million copies in its first four years, and sometime in the 1970s surpassed two million copies. For one six-month period, José Iturbi received the largest check up to that point RCA Victor had ever cut for royalties: $118,000.

Iturbi was born in Valencia, Spain, in 1895. His mother and father were reportedly at a performance of *Carmen* when she went into labor. He was a child prodigy on the piano, and became a pianist at the silent movie theater in Valencia, Cinema Turia, when he was seven years old. He also taught piano to students who were older than he was. He worked his way through school, studying in Paris at the Conservatory. He moved to Switzerland with his family, where he taught piano at Geneva's Conservatory, a position held by Liszt in 1835. Because he was so strict about technique, the students there called him "The Spanish Inquisition." After becoming a widower, he moved to the United States in 1929, making a storied debut under the baton of Leopold Stokowski. Iturbi toured, returned to Paris now and then, and began conducting. He premiered Beethoven's Ninth Symphony in Mexico. He took up flying as a hobby and became fairly obsessed with it.

When the United States entered World War II in 1941, he hoped to join the U.S. Army Air Corps, but he was already forty-five years old. He joined in the war effort post-1941, playing USO shows, and also flew for the Civil Air Patrol as Major Iturbi. It was the war effort that finally convinced him to work for Hollywood. He had avoided it, but changed his mind when his friend, successful film producer Joe Pasternak, suggested it would be good for morale. Iturbi played piano in seven films, using his skills as a classical composer, but also showed versatility by playing boogie-woogie, jazz, and honky-tonk. He continued concertizing, recording, and conducting into his late 1970s, and died in the summer of 1980, a few months shy of his eighty-fifth birthday.

One of the film's biggest fans was pianist Liberace. According to Larry Kart's obituary of popular pianist Liberace (*Chicago Tribune*), the trademark candelabra he kept on his piano was inspired by one in *A Song to Remember*. Also, among Liberace's many pianos was the green Pleyel piano used in the film. Liberace was known to perform a few pieces by Chopin in his act. In addition to medleys on the Minute Waltz and Polonaise, his signature Chopin piece was the Nocturne in E-flat major.

A Song to Remember is just one of a trend of biographical films (with varying degrees of veracity) about composers. After *Song to Remember* came *The Magic Bow* (1946), a film about virtuoso violinist Niccolò Paganini. A biopic about composer Robert Schumann followed in 1947. *Song of Love* featured the forbidden romance of Clara Schumann, beautifully played by Katharine Hepburn, and Robert Schumann, played by Paul Henreid. The screenplay was based on a play, *Song of Love, the Life of Robert and Clara Schumann* by Bernard Schubert and Mario Silva. This particular film focused on Clara's loving support even as Robert has a mental breakdown and deteriorates. Just as *A Song to Remember* drew upon patriotic themes, *Song of Love* seems to connect to the issues many families felt with the return of veterans from World War II. These themes were tackled explicitly in films like *The Best Years of Our Lives*, which was both a commercial and critical success, winning seven Academy Awards.

Also in 1947, there was *Song of Scheherazade*, a biopic about Russian composer Rimsky-Korsakov. This film was more escapist, with exotic locations and music inspired by foreign lands like Rimsky-Korsakov's "Song of India," *Capriccio Espagnol*, and of course the titular *Scheherazade*. Film music scholar Mervyn Cooke said of these kinds of films: "Many of these pictures concentrated on the composers' love lives, thereby cementing the longstanding association between musical romanticism and diegetic love-interest."

More of these films followed in the second half of the twentieth century including the Liszt biopic *Song Without End* (1960), like *A Song to Remember*, directed by Charles Vidor (with help from an uncredited George Cukor). A biopic about Edvard Grieg, *Song of Norway*, followed in 1970. Also in the 1970s, Academy Award–winner Ken Russell, who directed The Who's rock opera, *Tommy*, came out with a trio of musical biopics that stretched the established style of the genre. Cutting his teeth on controversial BBC documentaries about Sir Edward Elgar, Claude Debussy, and Richard Strauss (which implied involvement with the Nazis, so the Strauss family pulled rights to the music), Russell took to the big screen with the Tchaikovsky film *The Music Lovers* (1970), *Mahler* (1974), and *Lisztomania* (1975), which featured The Who frontman, Roger Daltrey. These works were more

interested in style over substance, and less about the lives of the composers involved. These were not meant to be mainstream films. A *Song
to Remember* seems rather innocent in comparison. Although it was not
the first film to depict aspects of the life of a composer, it fits into the
pantheon of composer biopics. Chopin's life would again be the subject
of film in the 1990s and 2000s.

CHOPIN ON FILM, PART 2: THE FEMININE MAN

The George Sand of *A Song to Remember* is a beautiful, strong woman,
whose refined exterior masks a harsh, uncompromising personality. She
would rather Chopin be true to his individuality than sacrifice his art
and his life for the greater good. The George Sand of 1991's *Impromptu*
deals less with Chopin's sense of duty than his frail physical nature. In
fact, much is made of the gender-bending aspect of the love story, with
George in the stereotypical male role and Chopin as the "woman" to be
wooed. There are love triangles and gossip and artists hiding from each
other in closets. There is the element of farce at times, but it is also
quite a modern take on the story. Critic Janet Maslin in her *New York
Times* review described the film as so "merrily and unapologetically
contemporary that all of these events might easily be taking place in the
present day."

The focus of the film is on George Sand herself. The opening shot is
of George as a little girl (Aurora): idealistic, adventurous, yearning for
perfect love, and ready to swear if it doesn't go her way. As an adult, she
strides confidently into her publisher's office, wearing men's clothes,
and smoking. With her clothes and plain speech, she causes a stir everywhere she goes. The film builds a love triangle with George and two of
her former lovers, Félicien Mallefille, her children's tutor, and Alfred
De Musset, the poet. De Musset, who has been tossed aside by George,
has a harsh view of her, saying: "She's a cannibal. She would drink the
blood of her children from the skull of her lover and not feel so much as
a stomachache."

The Chopin of *Impromptu* (played by Hugh Grant) has a delicate
cough that he hides behind white gloves. He is described as "frail as a
holy wafer." He is soft-spoken, unfailingly polite, and always perfectly
dressed. In the very first scene of him, visiting with Franz Liszt, he is

shutting the window against the summer dust. Liszt is playing his Transcendental Étude "Mazeppa," and Chopin in turn demonstrates his Ballade No. 1. George is visiting Liszt's mistress, the Countess Marie d'Agoult and listening to Liszt and Chopin play in the other room. Chopin remains somewhat mysterious to her for the first half hour of the film. She hears his music, but misses actually meeting him.

Hearing that Chopin, Liszt, and Marie d'Agoult have been invited to a count's estate in Angers, George invites herself along. Avoiding De Musset and Mallefille, she sneaks into Chopin's room to hear the Ballade in G minor that he is playing. When he stops, she startles him. Noting her trousers, he knows who she is. He says, "Madame Sand, rumor has it you are a woman and so I must ask you to leave my private chambers." When she asks to hear one more piece of music, he calls her actions, "ridiculously improper and frightening as well." When she finally leaves she proclaims that he's "not a man at all; you're an angel." Countess Marie d'Agoult (Liszt's mistress, played by Bernadette Peters) echoes this when she counsels George on how to "win" Chopin. "I know the man. He is not a man. He's a woman. He's all emotion and refinement. He has very few defenses. You must win him as a man wins a woman."

In taking this advice, a montage follows of George on horseback, riding alongside Chopin's carriage and gallantly tipping her hat to him. Chopin receives a large bouquet of flowers at home from George, and having fittings at the same haberdashery, George encounters Chopin getting fitted for a new coat (the same coat that George walks out with). The montage is set to Chopin's Étude in E minor, known as the "Wrong Note" Étude (op. 25, no. 5). It fades out, as Chopin says, "She has the most alarming way of turning up everywhere I go." D'Agoult causes conflict with gossip, but the truth comes out eventually. The two finally become lovers after Mallefille and Chopin duel—the composer faints and Sand shoots her former lover. Now alone, with no more obstacles to their relationship, Sand wants to consummate their physical romance, but Chopin explains:

> I'm so ill, and I have been for such a long time. And my body is such a great disappointment to me that I've already said goodbye to it. I'm not really in it anymore. I'm just happier floating about in music. And if I should come back inside this miserable collection of bones then I am afraid that it would probably collapse all together.

The physical heartiness and self-assuredness of Sand is held up against the frail and delicate Chopin. "Take my strength," she says to him. "I have too much of it." The film ends at the beginning of this long-term relationship, with nothing but potential and promise ahead.

CHOPIN ON FILM, PART 3: PETULANT ARTIST

The Americans had their chance to immortalize Chopin on film and did so in the 1940s to show off his work as a patriot. He dies at the end, tragically, although in self-sacrifice for his homeland. In the 1990s, the British–French production of *Impromptu* had fun with love triangles, scandal, and gender stereotypes. The ending of the film is happy, as his relationship with George Sand is at its promising beginning. In the Polish production *Chopin: Desire for Love* (2002), we see Chopin re-cast again, and perhaps not in the most favorable light. It is notable that this film, called *Chopin. Pragnienie miłości* in its original language, chooses to portray a version of Chopin that is sometimes selfish and cold, a musical genius, but a frustrated human being, needing to be at the center of someone's attention. One can hardly imagine Cornel Wilde or Hugh Grant screaming and yelling in the way that actor Piotr Adamczyk does in this film.

The film has two versions, one in Polish and one in English. The latter used British actors to dub over the dialogue. The director Jerzy Antczak wrote the screenplay with wife Jadwiga Barańska (who also played Chopin's mother in the film), reportedly tinkering with the script for many years. The official site of the film explains the title: "A timeless story about our inability to understand each other and our desperate desire for love. . . . A tangled web of unruly passion lies at the center of this drama, chronicling the stormy affair between the great piano virtuoso Fryderyk Chopin and the flamboyant feminist writer Aurore Dupin, who called herself George Sand." Kevin Thomas of the *Los Angeles Times* described the film as "a persuasive portrait of an artistic household so tempestuous as to be draining to witness." Thomas astutely describes this version of Chopin as "petulant."

The film covers the time from Chopin's emigration from Warsaw to his death, but focuses mainly on the ten-year relationship of Chopin and George Sand. As in *A Song to Remember*, *Desire for Love* dramatizes a moment in which Liszt—already famous—uses his notoriety to help Chopin break through in Paris society.

The film opens with Chopin being woken in the middle of the night to play for the mad Archduke Constantine. The archduke rules by fear, and is portrayed as brutal and unhinged. Chopin protests, but his father insists, saying that the archduke might help him get a scholarship. He arrives and Constantine is playing the march that Chopin wrote for him. It is implied that Constantine has an unhealthy affection for Chopin. In reminding Chopin of their first meeting, when Chopin was just seven years old, he says, "I still keep the memory of your beautiful eyes. . . . I loved you even before you started to play." It is his volatility, and this suggested abuse, that urges Chopin to leave Warsaw. No mention is made of Chopin's first trips abroad, and when he leaves it's as if he's leaving for the first time.

Like the Sand of *Impromptu*, actress Danuta Stenka's George Sand tries at first to woo Chopin with gifts and flowers. In the end, it is the denial of his marriage proposal to Maria Wodzińska that finally convinces Chopin to begin his relationship with Sand. There is the added issue of Félicien Mallefille, Sand's former lover, who threatens them. In this film, Chopin's friend Albert [Grzymata] takes care of the threat by sending Mallefille away. Chopin, Sand, and her children travel to Mallorca for the winter of 1838–1839. This is the central part of the film, with their initial happiness dissolving into numerous problems: the cold and rainy weather, the lodging problems of the Carthusian monastery (no heat, leaks), the poor quality of the piano sent to Chopin, the dislike of the scandalized Catholic population of the island, Chopin's poor health, and the conflict between Chopin and Maurice Sand. It is in fact this latter relationship that causes the most trouble. Sand attempts to balance her time between her children and her lover. The men in particular are at war for her attention, and she ends up disappointing both of them. In the film, Chopin takes ill during their trip to Mallorca and is diagnosed with galloping consumption. The balancing act attempted by Sand becomes even more precarious, as she must tend to Chopin's health needs as well as his emotional needs.

There are numerous scenes of Maurice (Adam Woronowicz) being driven mad by Chopin's presence. Sand attempts to encourage Maurice's painting, and even tries to get Chopin to give his opinion on Maurice's art. Instead, Chopin can only complain about the piano in their lodgings. Maurice feels Chopin is selfish; Chopin thinks Maurice is rude. After their return to Sand's country estate in Nohant, the relationship between Sand and Chopin transitions into a platonic friendship. Sand sees this as the natural evolution of their partnership, while Chopin is certain that it must be his disease that drives her away. She encourages him to stay at Nohant and continue his work. A new conflict arrives when daughter Solange (Bozena Stachura) begins flirting with Chopin. She begins to see herself as a romantic prospect for his affections. When Chopin spurns her advances, she attempts to win him through her youthful beauty. It is implied that Chopin is having an affair with one of the servants at Nohant, and this causes more problems between Chopin and Solange. Sand tries to explain that Chopin "loves nothing but his music." Maurice attempts suicide. The presence of Chopin in their lives has torn the family apart. At a tense dinner, Chopin leaves the table in annoyance because he was served the wrong part of the chicken. It is this slight that Chopin uses as an excuse to leave Nohant. When Chopin departs, their goodbye is civil.

Back in Paris, Solange becomes engaged to sculptor Jean-Baptiste Clésinger. This causes a break between Solange and her mother. Chopin sides with Solange in the conflict, and Sand assumes that this means Chopin and Solange are having an affair. Chopin and Sand meet by chance, and Chopin tells Sand of the birth of Solange's daughter. Chopin's health declines, and he writes a letter to his family, asking for them to come to him. It will be his final illness. At his bedside is his sister Ludwika, who accedes to his request that his heart return to Warsaw. The film ends with her crossing the border back into Poland, narrowly avoiding search by the border guard.

A theme that keeps recurring is Chopin imagining scenes as his music plays, suggesting that he was rendering these activities—a carriage ride in a storm, a beautiful woman running through a field—into musical form. When his servant plays a folk tune on his violin, Chopin uses it as the basis of a polonaise and he imagines a festive party outdoors, with people dancing, brightly colored skirts on the women, and lots of laughter. It is a rare moment of joy for the sullen Chopin.

Although the focus is more about the many conflicts of Chopin's relationships, the music in the film is still quite important, and beautifully done. Marta Broczkowska was the music supervisor. Also involved in the production were pianists Janusz (Jerzy) Olejniczak, Emanuel Ax, and Yukio Yokoyama, cellist Yo-Yo Ma, and violinists Vadim Brodski and Pamela Frank. Orchestrations were done by Wojciech Gogolewski, Jerzy Maksymiuk, and Henryk Kuźniak.

IMPROMPTUS AND WALTZES

In the film *Impromptu*, Chopin plays George Sand part of his Fantasie-Impromptu, one of four he composed in this genre. It was written in 1834, one of the pieces from Chopin's first years in Paris. The dedicatee was Julian Fontana, fellow Polish composer and pianist. Fontana, who was Chopin's musical executor, published the work only after Chopin's death. It is impetuous and striking, and the opening section and the closing are quite quick. The middle section provides a respite with a lovely *Largo* melody. It is this tune that briefly appears at the end, almost like a memory of the melody's ephemeral beauty.

Hugh Grant's Chopin explains the idea behind an impromptu, which has a name that implies it springs from the mind without planning: "A perfect impromptu *sounds* spontaneous and free. No one should be able to guess at all the desperate calculation behind it." He goes on to hint why this particular piece should have seen the light of day only after Chopin's death: "I have been struggling with it for so long. It's like being tangled in a net, I feel. I have terrible dreams at night. Well, I think if I ever finish it that then it will have finished me."

Chopin composed three other impromptus, and all are one-movement, multi-sectional pieces. The first, op. 29, was composed in 1837. It has three sections with the two outer parts in A-flat major and a contrasting section in the middle of F minor. Its quick tempo and continuous figuration in the hands makes it quite a challenge. Impromptu No. 2, op. 36 was composed two years later. Chopin chose the key of F-sharp major, and again, Chopin constructed a complex work. His gift for melody shines in this particular piece. The third impromptu, op. 51, was composed in 1843, which was actually his last composed, but not the last one published. He dedicated this piece to one of his pupils, and it was clearly one of his favorite pieces to play because he programmed it on more than one of his rare public performances. In the contrasting middle section, Chopin achieves a great effect by switching the melody to the left hand while the right plays the accompaniment.

The origins of the waltz date back to the mid-1700s. The German word "walzen" means to roll or turn, and this word in connection with dance began to appear about 1750. Dances described by the term had two main things in common: the music that accompanied them was in triple time, and the formation of the dancers was a close couple embrace. Dances of this type were popular in Germany, Bavaria, Bohemia, and Austria and went by many different descriptive names like the Ländler. As these types of dances became popular, filtering into high society, controversy followed. After all, the waltz allowed couples to share an intimate embrace in public. Also, there were reports of dizziness and breathlessness among waltzers.

Chopin began writing waltzes in 1824, when he was a teenager in Poland. At first he didn't consider the waltz a serious art form. Chopin's waltzes, which were meant more for seated audiences than dancers, achieved an artfulness that elevated the form. In addition to the waltzes he must have heard while living in Vienna, Chopin may have also been influenced by German composer Carl Maria von Weber, who wrote a concert work based on the waltz called *Invitation to the Dance*.

Chopin published just eight waltzes when he was alive, but wrote many more. Five more were published in 1855, and one more came to light in 1868. There were more that were catalogued, but many of those have been lost, including half a dozen that Chopin's sister had in her house when it burned down. All convey the 3/4 time associated with the waltz, but some have quick tempos and dance-like moods, while some display a melancholy and pensive character. Like many dance forms, the waltzes often consisted of distinctive sixteen-bar melodies that were repeated. Chopin sometimes embellished this form, and sometimes kept it simple. The dramatic shifts within one waltz could be quite affecting.

The "Minute" Waltz is one of Chopin's most popular works, and has made appearances in cartoons and films. In *A Song to Remember*, it forms the transitional piece from Chopin's childhood to his maturity. In *Impromptu*, when George Sand asks for a minute of Chopin's attention, he times her with this waltz. Chopin did not actually mean for it to be performed in a minute, he actually meant it the way Bugs Bunny pronounces it, which would mean small, miniature. Chopin biographers

Camille Bourniquel and Niecks mention that Chopin was inspired to write this piece as he watched Sand's dog Marquis chase his tail at Nohant. Chopin first called it the "Little Dog Waltz." It was one of three Chopin composed for a small collection published by Breitkopf & Härtel in 1847. He dedicated this waltz to Delfina Potocka. It is constructed in an ABA form, with the second A section extended only slightly. The lyrical B section appears as a work young Chopin presents to his teacher in *A Song to Remember*. It was a part of his last public concert in 1848. There is also a popular version with lyrics added by Lan O'Kun. It was performed by Barbara Streisand on her album *Color Me Barbara* (1966).

CHOPIN THE VIDEO GAME CHARACTER

Our final portrayals of Chopin are arguably the most unique. In the 2007 video game *Eternal Sonata*, Chopin is the central character of a role-playing game, and he is also the protagonist of 2014's *Frederic: Resurrection of Music*. The actions of *Eternal Sonata* take place in the dream world experienced by Chopin as he dies of tuberculosis. The director of the game, Hiroya Hatsushiba, described his desire to bring attention to Chopin's music by creating a fantasy world in which gamers would experience classical music as part of the action. Hatsushiba has said: "By creating a colorful fantasy world in Chopin's dream, I was hoping that people would get into this game easily and also come to know how great Chopin's music is." There are numerous compositions used in the game, some played by pianist Stanislav Bunin, and original music and orchestrations by composer Motoi Sakuraba.

The first appearance of Chopin is during the introduction. It is October 16, 1849. Chopin lies in bed, watched over by a doctor and a woman, perhaps his sister Ludwika. Another female friend sits close by, possibly Delfina Potocka. This scene of "reality" returns a few times. He appears later as a character in the game, dressed in a fancy coat and top hat. One can play and battle as Chopin, but a player can also act as other members of the party. It is revealed that only those close to death can use magic. Chopin has the power, but so does a young woman named Polka, who has been shunned by the people in her town because they think she's contagious. Chopin believes that Polka's world has grown out of his imagination, but there is some ambiguity about that.

The characters and places all have musical names. The small village is called Tenuto, and the larger town is Ritardando. Two young men are also playable characters named Allegretto (called Retto for short) and Beat. There is a shepherd named Viola (who has a dog named Arco), and a revolutionary named Jazz who leads a group called Andantino. In an interlude between chapters of the game, Chopin's "Raindrop" Prelude plays, and real pictures (a montage in a computer game known as a cutscene) of Paris and Mallorca accompany subtitles about the romance between Chopin and George Sand, and about the genesis of this piece. The game continues with multiple members joining the party (most of them playable characters) as they set off on a quest of both peace and social justice. When Chopin is finally defeated, Polka sacrifices herself for him. In the "real" world, Chopin dies; the doctor calls his time of death as two o'clock in the morning.

The scene that opened the game—featuring a younger version of Polka and her mother—returns, although this time we hear Chopin's voice speaking over the original dialogue. He calls the fourteen-year-old version of Polka back to life, and she reappears, hugging Allegretto. Back in Chopin's room, his spirit rises from his body and plays one final piece on the piano. It's a new piece, inspired by Polka (composed by Motoi Sakuraba) and sung by the Delfina Potocka character. It is an aria called "Heaven's Mirror," a title inspired by a certain kind of flower—encountered by Chopin and Polka upon their first meeting—that bloom in the darkness of night.

The game sold well and garnered critical acclaim and awards, including best score on an Xbox 360 game in 2007. In a review of the game, IGN describes the central premise as follows: "In a land where music influences both combat and exploration, Chopin sets out on a journey not only of self-discovery, but also one of redemption." Another review praises the educational angle of the game saying:

> The game puts you in the role of a historical figure. In doing so, it teaches music appreciation and history. . . . It uses [Chopin's] music and life to bring context to what is happening in front of you. The themes, events and motivations for characters have correlations with Chopin's real life.

Although the majority of music in the game is newly composed, there are seven works by Chopin on the *Eternal Sonata* soundtrack.

The music of Chopin is more central to the concept of *Frederic: Resurrection of Music* from Forever Entertainment. The game, which is played in an app compatible with Mac devices, explores the return of the composer Chopin to a world full of thoughtless, soulless pop music. Chopin is called to rise from the grave after 165 years to fight musical battles against modern musicians. It's unclear who has brought Chopin back for these battles, but that emerges as the overarching mystery of the game. Three Muses appear to offer their help to the disoriented composer who finds himself in a noisy modern version of Paris he doesn't understand. They tell him: "Since you left, no master has appeared," and offer him two tools: a magic chariot and a grand piano. The player of this game must "play" remixed versions of nine of Chopin's works. A keyboard appears at the bottom of the screen and musical notes travel down to the keys. The player must tap these notes in the proper rhythm. The gameplay has a similar idea to other popular games like *Guitar Hero* and *Rock Band*. Chopin is challenged at first by Jean, a French musician who has numerous synthesizers and writes electronic music. He threatens to defeat and "sample" Chopin. If one plays Chopin's music accurately enough, the challengers are destroyed. The first work that appears is an electronic remix of the Prelude in E minor, op. 28, no. 4. In subsequent challenges, the Polonaise in A major op. 40, no. 1 appears in reggae style, the Funeral March is reimagined as a country tune, and the Étude in G-flat major op. 25, no. 9 is remixed as an Irish jig. When Chopin is in New York, he battles with a combination of the Polonaise in A-flat major, op. 53 and the Nocturne in F minor op. 55, no. 1.

Who could have guessed that nearly two centuries after Chopin was born that he would be immortalized as a character in not one, but two video games? In this, and in so many other ways, Chopin's music endures. It is heartening to think that Chopin's life and music could inspire something so twenty-first century as an RPG or an app, and we should be hopeful that such inspiration will continue in the coming years.

GLOSSARY

accompaniment. The part of the musical composition that harmonically supports the melody.

arpeggio. A chord with its notes played in succession rather than simultaneously.

arrangement. A version of a musical piece adapted in some way from its original iteration.

cantabile. An expression that directs a performer to render something "in a singing fashion."

character piece. A broad term for a short (usually) solo piano piece based on a single idea.

chord. A group of three or more pitches sounded simultaneously, usually to create harmony.

chromaticism. The use of some pitches in a musical composition that don't belong to the original key.

concerto. A musical composition which features a solo instrument (or small group of instruments) supported by a larger group—usually an orchestra in order to show the contrast between the two entities.

counterpoint. A musical texture in which multiple independent melodies interact.

dissonance. The resulting clash when two or more notes do not sound harmonious together.

dynamics. The degree of loudness or softness of a musical composition or phrase.

étude. A musical piece for solo instrument constructed to build technique, develop expression, or display skill.

harpsichord. The dominant keyboard instrument in the sixteenth to the eighteenth century in Europe; sound is produced when a player hits a key and a plectrum plucks a string inside; dynamic range was negligible.

interval. The distance between two notes.

legato. Manner of performance in which the player maintains a sense of connection among the notes of the phrase; in a smooth and connected fashion.

melody. A musical phrase that is the dominant line in a musical texture and which feels musically complete.

motive. A short musical idea that is repeated and expanded upon throughout a musical piece.

octave. A span of eight notes.

pedal. Foot-operated levers on a piano; modern grands have three.

polyrhythm. Two or more rhythms sounding simultaneously.

program music. Instrumental music that is inspired by some extra-musical idea or narrative.

Romanticism. A movement in art, literature, and music that arose around the turn of the nineteenth century which was characterized by expression, emotion, and individuality.

rondo. A musical form in which there is a phrase or section that continually returns.

rubato. A musical term that indicates a flexibility in rhythm to speed up or slow down as the emotional expression warrants.

scale. A succession of notes organized around a fundamental pitch or pattern.

scherzo. A light, sometimes fast musical composition that developed from the minuet movement of symphonies.

soirée. A lively gathering at a home, usually one in which there will be a musical performance.

texture. The interaction of musical lines in a piece and the resulting density; a polyphonic texture indicates that there are many musical lines all working somewhat independently, while monophonic works are made up of a single melody line with no accompaniment.

transcription. An arrangement of a musical piece adapted into a new medium, as in a piano transcription of a string quartet.

virtuosity. A display of skill that demonstrates a level of mastery far beyond most players.

virtuoso. In music, a performer who demonstrates an extremely high level of skill.

SELECTED READING

Atwood, William G. *Fryderyk Chopin: Pianist from Warsaw*. New York: Columbia University Press, 1987.

Azoury, Pierre. *Chopin Through His Contemporaries: Friends, Lovers, and Rivals*. Westport, CT: Greenwood Press, 1999.

Bach, C. P. E. *Essay on the True Art of Playing Keyboard Instruments* [1753]. Trans. William J. Mitchell. New York: W. W. Norton, 1949.

Cortot, Alfred. *In Search of Chopin*. Trans. Cyril and Rena Clarke. Westport, CT: Greenwood Press, 1975.

Bomberger, E. Douglas, et al. "The Piano Lesson." In *Piano Roles: A New History of the Piano*. James Parakilas, ed. New Haven, CT: Yale University Press, 2002.

Duchen, Jessica. "Pauline Viardot: The Forgotten Diva." http://www.independent.co.uk/arts-entertainment/music/features/pauline-viardot-the-forgotten-diva-6108586.html. Accessed 12 November 2016.

Duchen, Jessica. "Sex and Chopin." *The Guardian*. (10 September 1999). http://www.jessicaduchen.co.uk/pdfs/guardian-pdfs/1999/10-9-99-sexand_chopin.pdf. Accessed 3 November 2015.

Ehrlich, Cyril. *The Piano: A History*. London: J.M. Dent and Sons, Ltd. 1976.

Eigeldinger, Jean-Jacques. *Chopin: Pianist and Teacher: As Seen By His Pupils*. Trans. Naomi Shohet, with Krysia Osostowicz, and Roy Howat. Cambridge, UK: Cambridge University Press, 1988.

Eisler, Benita. *Chopin's Funeral*. New York: Vintage Books, 2003.

Fryderyk Chopin Society. Chopin.pl., www.chopin.pl. Accessed 4 October 2016.

Gołab, Maciej. *Twelve Studies in Chopin: Style, Aesthetics and Reception*. Trans. Wojciech Bońkowski, John Comber, and Maksymilian Kapelański. Frankfurt am Main: Peter Lang, 2014.

Harley, Maria Anna. "Chopin and Women Composers: Collaborations, Imitations, Inspirations." *The Polish Review*. v45 n1 (2000): 29–50. http://www.jstor.org/stable/25779170. Accessed 12 November 2016.

Hedley, Arthur. *Chopin*. London: J.M. Dent, 1974.

Higgins, Thomas. "Delphine Potocka and Frederic Chopin." *Journal of the American Liszt Society* n8 (1980): 64–74; n9 (1981): 73–87.

Hilmes, Oliver. *Franz Liszt: Musician, Celebrity, Superstar*. Trans. Stewart Spencer. New Haven, CT: Yale University Press, 2016.

Huneker, James. *Chopin: The Man and His Music*. New York: Scribner 1900; Reprint, New York: Dover, 1966.

Jordan, Ruth. *Nocturne: A Life of Chopin*. New York: Taplinger Publishing Company, 1978.

Kallberg, Jeffrey. *Chopin at the Boundaries: Sex, History, and Musical Genre.* Cambridge, MA: Harvard University Press, 1996.

Karenberg, Axel. "Chopin's Misery and Musicians' Medical Biography." *Sudhoffs Archiv*, Bd. 91, H. 1 (2007): 82–98.

Kelley, Edgar Stillman. *Chopin the Composer: His Structural Art and Its Influence on Contemporaneous Music.* New York: G. Schirmer, 1913; Reprint, New York: Cooper Square, 1969.

Kizińska, Karolina. "Women Composers: As Emerging from the Shadows." *Mea Kultura.* http://meakultura.pl/publikacje/women-composers-as-emerging-from-the-shadows-310. Accessed 28 September 2016.

Kuzemko, J. A. "Chopin's Illnesses." *Journal of the Royal Society of Medicine* v87 (December 1994): 769–772.

Lawlor, Clark. *Consumption and Literature: The Making of the Romantic Disease.* Houndsmill, Basingstoke, Hampshire: Palgrave Macmillan, 2006.

Lederer, Victor. *Chopin: A Listener's Guide to the Master of the Piano.* Milwaukee, WI: Amadeus Press, 2006.

Liszt, Franz. *Life of Chopin.* Trans. Martha Walker Cook. New York: Dover Publications, 2005.

Majka, Lucyna, Joanna Goździk, and Michał Witt. "Cystic Fibrosis—A Probable Cause of Frédéric Chopin's Suffering and Death." *Journal of Applied Genetics* v44 n1 (2003): 77–84.

Marek, George R., and Maria Gordon-Smith. *Chopin.* New York: Harper & Row Publishers, 1978.

Maurois, Andre. *Lelia: The Life of George Sand.* New York: Penguin Books, 1977.

Narodowy Instytut Fryderyka Chopina/The Fryderyk Chopin Institute (NIFC). en.chopin.nifc.pl/chopin/main/page. Accessed 4 August 2016.

Opieński, Henryk, ed. *Chopin's Letters.* Trans. Ethel Lilian Voynich. New York: Knopf, 1931; Reprint, New York: Dover Publications, 1988.

Plantinga, Leon, B. *Schumann as Critic.* New Haven, CT: Yale University Press, 1967.

Plantinga, Leon. *Clementi: His Life and Music.* New York: Oxford University Press, 1977.

Rosen, Charles. *The Romantic Generation.* Cambridge, MA: Harvard University Press, 1995.

Samson, Jim, ed. *Chopin Studies.* Cambridge, UK: Cambridge University Press, 1988.

Samson, Jim. *Chopin: The Four Ballades.* Cambridge, UK: Cambridge University Press, 1992.

Samson, Jim, and Kornel Michałowski. "Chopin, Fryderyk Franciszek." In Stanley Sadie and John Tyrell, eds., *The New Grove Dictionary of Music and Musicians*, 2nd ed. London: Macmillan, 2001, v5: 706–736.

Sand, George. *Correspondence.* George Lubin, ed. Paris: Éditions Garnier Frères, 1964–1971; 8 vols.

Sand, George. *Lucrezia Floriani.* Trans. Julius Eker. Chicago: Chicago Review Press, 1993.

Sand, George. *Story of My Life: The Autobiography of George Sand.* Thelma Jurgrau, ed. Albany: State University of New York Press, 1991.

Sand, George. *Winter in Mallorca.* Trans. and annot. Robert Graves. London: Cassell, 1956.

Schumann, Robert. *Music and Musicians: Essays and Criticisms.* Trans. Fanny Raymond Ritter. London: William Reeves, 1880.

Siepmann, Jeremy. *Chopin: The Reluctant Romantic.* Boston: Northeastern University Press, 1995.

Smialek, William, and Maja Trochimczyk. *Frédéric Chopin: A Research and Information Guide*, 2nd ed. New York: Routledge, 2015.

Solie, Ruth, ed. *Musicology and Difference: Gender and Sexuality in Music Scholarship.* Berkeley, CA: University of California Press, 1995.

Swinkin, Jeffrey. "Keyboard Fingering and Interpretation: A Comparison of Historical and Modern Approaches." *Performance Practice Review*: v12 n1, Article 1 (2007). http://scholarship.claremont.edu/ppr/vol12/iss1/1. Accessed 12 November 2016.

Szulc, Tad. *Chopin in Paris: The Life and Times of the Romantic Composer.* New York: Scribner, 1998.

Todd, Larry, ed. *Nineteenth-Century Piano Music*. New York: Schirmer Books, 1990.

Tsioulcas, Anastasia. "Uncovering the Heart of Chopin—Literally." NPR.org. (17 November 2014). http://www.npr.org/sections/deceptivecadence/2014/11/17/364756853/uncovering-the-heart-of-chopin-literally. Accessed 7 October 2015.

Witten, David. "The Coda Wagging the Dog: Tails and Wedges in the Chopin Ballades." In Larry Todd, ed., *Nineteenth-Century Piano Music: Essays in Performance and Analysis*. New York: Schirmer Books, 1990.

Wierzynski, Casimir. *The Life and Death of Chopin*. New York: Simon & Schuster, 1949.

SELECTED LISTENING

CD

Ballades. Murray Perahia. Sony Classical, 1995.
Ballades. Evgeny Kissin. Sony Classical, 1999.
Études. Maurizio Pollini. Deutsche Grammaphon, 1985.
Études. Alfred Cortot. Naxos, 2006.
Études. Claudio Arrau. EMI Classics France, 1990.
Mazurkas. Vladimir Ashkenazy. Decca, 1996.
Mazurkas. Vladimir Horowitz. Sony Classical, 2003.
Nocturnes. Artur Rubinstein. Sony Classical, 2000 (remaster).
Nocturnes. Dang Thai Son. Imports, 2014.
Piano Concertos. Martha Argerich and the Montreal Symphony Orchestra conducted by Charles Dutoit. EMI, 1999.
Piano Concertos. Maria Joao Pires and the Royal Philharmonic Orchestra conducted by Andre Previn. Deutsche Grammaphon, 2013.
Polonaises. Artur Rubinstein. Naxos, 2010 (remaster).
Preludes. Claudio Arrau. Philips, 2007.
Sonatas. Janina Fialkowska. ATMA, 2010.
Waltzes. Dinu Lipatti. EMI Classics, 1950 (remastered 1999).
Waltzes. Vladimir Ashkenazy. Decca, 1987.

Chopin Complete Edition. Deutsche Grammaphon, 2009. 17-CD anthology of various performers including Arrau, Pollini, and Zimerman.

The Real Chopin. Complete Works of Fryderyk Chopin on Period Instruments. Warsaw: NIFC, 2010. 21-CD set featuring various performers on period instruments: 1849 Erard and 1848 Pleyel.

DVD

Chopin: Desire for Love. Directed by Jerzy Antczak. American World Pictures, 2005.
Impromptu. Directed by James Lapine. MGM Home Entertainment, 1991.
In Search of Chopin. Directed by Phil Grabsky. Seventh Art, 2014.
In the Footsteps of Chopin. Directed by Yves Henry. Kultur Studios. 2012.
The Pianist. Directed by Roman Polanski. Universal Studios Home Entertainment, 2006.
A Song to Remember. Directed by Charles Vidor. Mill Creek Entertainment, 1945.
The Strange Case of Delfina Potocka. Directed by Tony Palmer. Tony Palmer Films, 2010.

VIDEO GAMES

Eternal Sonata. Directed by Hiroya Hatsushiba. Bandai Namco Games, 2007.
Chopin: Resurrection of Music. Forever Entertainment, 2014.

INDEX

ABOUT THE AUTHOR

Christine Lee Gengaro is an educator, writer, and musician based in Los Angeles. Her first book, *Listening to Stanley Kubrick: The Music in His Films*, was published by Scarecrow Press in 2013. She received her PhD in historical musicology from University of Southern California in 2005. A tenured professor of music at Los Angeles City College for the last ten years, she teaches music theory, voice, and music history. An avid writer and scholar, she has presented papers in the United States, Europe, and Malaysia, and her published articles on film music and classical music in media appear in numerous journals and books. She has written program notes for the *Mozartwoche* concert series in Vienna, the Ford Theatre Foundation, the St. Paul Chamber Orchestra, Camerata Pacifica, and has been program annotator and blogger for the Los Angeles Chamber Orchestra since 2007. Passionate about education, she is also involved with LACO's outreach program, which serves elementary school students in Los Angeles. She is currently annotating and editing a new edition of Anthony Burgess's *This Man and Music*.

CPSIA information can be obtained
at www.ICGtesting.com
Printed in the USA
BVOW06*0951101217
501741BV00006B/4/P